"I've written a lot of books and read even more, but once in a while I catch myself reading a great book from someone who has lived a great life, and I stop here and there, look out wistfully through an open window, and say, 'I wish I'd written that!' Wayne Cordeiro puts me in that kind of envious mood. But even if I had written *Jesus: Pure and Simple,* it would not have been done nearly as well. Because a book like *Jesus: Pure and Simple* can only come from the heart of a man who knows his subject very well. This is a book that might have been titled *Jesus Close Up.* After any single paragraph you will know it was written by a man who lives his devotion to the Savior, and out of the depths of his Christ-neediness makes the poor in spirit wealthy."

—Calvin Miller, speaker and author of *Letters to Heaven*
(and more than 70 other books)

"What I love about this book is that the content and title match what every follower of Christ should long for. In a world where everything soon gets over complicated, we all need these reminders to keep the main thing, the main thing—purity and simplicity of walking with Jesus every day."

—Doug Fields, speaker and author of *Fresh Start*

"To a generation that can't find the real story amidst all the tradition, churchyness, poor street cred, or newspaper headlines, *Jesus: Pure and Simple* is a breath of fresh air and should be the first place you start or start over."

—Hugh Halter, pastor and author of *Sacrilege*
and *The Tangible Kingdom*

"If you're sick, you need a doctor who knows how to study what's wrong with you and offer a savvy diagnosis—your life might depend on it. And in *Jesus: Pure and Simple*, Wayne Cordeiro is spot-on in his diagnosis of a Christian culture that is sick of itself. His prescription? More of Jesus, and less of everything else. I couldn't agree more."

—Rick Lawrence, longtime executive editor of *Group Magazine* and author of *Sifted* and *Shrewd*

JESUS

Books by Wayne Cordeiro

Jesus: Pure & Simple
Leading on Empty
The Divine Mentor
The Irresistible Church

JESUS

PURE & SIMPLE

WAYNE CORDEIRO

BETHANY HOUSE PUBLISHERS

a division of Baker Publishing Group
Minneapolis, Minnesota

© 2012 by Wayne Cordeiro

Published by Bethany House Publishers
11400 Hampshire Avenue South
Bloomington, Minnesota 55438
www.bethanyhouse.com

Bethany House Publishers is a division of
Baker Publishing Group, Grand Rapids, Michigan

Printed in the United States of America

ISBN 978-0-7642-0351-0 (hardcover)
ISBN 978-0-7642-1092-1 (pbk.)

Library of Congress Cataloging-in-Publication Data is available for this title: LCCN 2012028741.

Unless otherwise indicated, Scripture quotations are from the New American Standard Bible®, copyright © 1960, 1962, 1963, 1968, 1971, 1972, 1973, 1975, 1977, 1995 by The Lockman Foundation. Used by permission.

Scripture quotations identified ESV are from The Holy Bible, English Standard Version® (ESV®), copyright © 2001 by Crossway, a publishing ministry of Good News Publishers. Used by permission. All rights reserved. ESV Text Edition: 2007

Scripture quotations identified THE MESSAGE are from *The Message* by Eugene H. Peterson, copyright © 1993, 1994, 1995, 2000, 2001, 2002. Used by permission of NavPress Publishing Group. All rights reserved.

Scripture quotations identified NCV are from the New Century Version®. Copyright © 1987, 1988, 1991 by Word Publishing, a division of Thomas Nelson, Inc. Used by permission. All rights reserved.

Scripture quotations identified NIV are from the Holy Bible, New International Version®. NIV®. Copyright © 1973, 1978, 1984, 2011 by Biblica, Inc.™ Used by permission of Zondervan. All rights reserved worldwide. www.zondervan.com

Scripture quotations identified NKJV are from the New King James Version. Copyright © 1982 by Thomas Nelson, Inc. Used by permission. All rights reserved.

Scripture quotations identified NLT are from the *Holy Bible*, New Living Translation, copyright © 1996, 2004, 2007 by Tyndale House Foundation. Used by permission of Tyndale House Publishers, Inc., Carol Stream, Illinois 60188. All rights reserved.

The Internet addresses, email addresses, and phone numbers in this book are accurate at the time of publication. They are provided as a resource. Baker Publishing Group does not endorse them or vouch for their content or permanence.

Cover design by Lookout Design, Inc.

Author is represented by WordServe Literary Group.

12 13 14 15 16 17 18   7 6 5 4 3 2 1

CONTENTS

INTRODUCTION

When you cannot remember the 22 characteristics of a good wife, the 7 steps to authority, or the 9 ways of love . . .

It's time to get back to Jesus.

When a speaker insists (again) that you need to stop your bad habits, increase your devotion, reduce your worry, augment your faith, or banish your fears . . .

It's time to get back to Jesus.

When you're overwhelmed by testimonies of others praying all night, fasting forty days, raising the dead, and leading thousands to the Lord on their airplane rides home . . .

It's time to get back to Jesus.

When you've sat through your one hundred fifty millionth sermon about giving more, suffering more, doing more, or being more . . .

It's time to get back to Jesus.

When you attend another hyped-up conference that promises to be the one that will reduce all your problems, and you buy all the books and CDs and try them out, but nothing is reduced except your savings account . . .

It's time to get back to Jesus.

When someone points a finger in your face and says, "Thus saith the Lord," but their advice contradicts someone else who shouted a different "Thus saith the Lord," and *it* sounds different from yet *another* "Thus saith the Lord" . . .

It's time to get back to Jesus.

When your mailbox is flooded with a multitude of letters, newsletters, and giving requests from a multitude of organizations with three-initial names . . .

It's time to get back to Jesus.

It is time to hear His voice and simplify. It's time we get back to Jesus, pure and simple.[1]

That's what this book is all about.

---

1. Adapted from Jim May, *Living at His Place* (Lakewood, CO: Building on the Rock, 1995).

CHAPTER 1

PURE & SIMPLE

But I am afraid that, as the serpent deceived Eve by his craftiness, your minds will be led astray from the simplicity and purity
of devotion to Christ.

2 Corinthians 11:3

Nothing is as refreshing as a cold glass of fresh orange juice, *pure and simple*. For that matter, anything that is pure and simple is refreshing in today's artificial world of sleek packaging and million-dollar marketing. Currently there's a grassroots move-ment afoot for getting back to locally made and organically grown products. It could be a knee-jerk reaction to genetically modified vegetables using growth hormones and finished off with a touch of artificial green coloring, but I like it nevertheless.

A few weeks ago I read the label on a carton of apple juice, only to find that it was made with "10 percent real apple juice" (from concentrate, of course). I'll bet if I meandered down enough supermarket aisles, I'd one day find the small print on a carton of eggs to read "Eggs produced by synthetic chickens from Farmville. Assembled in China."

It's time to get back to the pure and simple.

One of my favorite passages in the Bible is 2 Corinthians 11:3. I memorized it early on, and it has become a safe haven for me when life spins out of control, which seems to happen more frequently as of late.

> But I am afraid that, as the serpent deceived Eve by his craftiness, your minds will be led astray from the simplicity and purity of devotion to Christ.
>
> 2 Corinthians 11:3

Here's something refreshing: a pure and simple devotion to Christ. Sounds wonderfully inviting, doesn't it?

And the good news is that it's not about doing more or doing less. Because God created you in His image, the more you become like Jesus, the more you become the person you were created to be. It is in Him that you actually find fulfillment, not in religious activities (as good as they may be) or in serene settings that give you a needed respite from your harried workplace. He is not the rest *from* our labors. He is the rest *in* our labors.

It's time to get back to the pure and simple.

"A promise remains of entering His rest" (Hebrews 4:1). It's the rest of a child close to his mother. It's the rest that comes when we are near the one we love. It's the rest we find when we are walking through unfamiliar surroundings with a guide who knows the way.

The closer you get to Jesus, the more at home you will feel in this journey. God designed it that way.

You have probably seen great influential Christian leaders in person or on television or listened to them on radio. You may have read their books and attended their conferences. In Jesus' day, Pharisees filled that bill. Gamaliel was one of the more popular ones. But even knowledgeable God-followers like Gamaliel missed the point. Read what Jesus said to a gathered group of them: "You search the Scriptures, for in them you think you have eternal life; and these are they which testify of Me. But you are not willing to come to Me that you may have life" (John 5:39–40 NKJV).

But missing the point may not mean that Jesus is distant. It's usually that our eyes are too full to see Him. Our attention is arrested by what commands our lives . . . this week's desires, today's fears, relationships we want, things we need, or problems we despise.

It's not destruction that causes our greatest concern.

It's *distraction*.

The Great Counterfeit

If you want to know what is valuable to God, check out what the devil counterfeits. Gaining a pure and simple relationship with Jesus is more counterfeited than Gucci sunglasses in China or Rolex watches in Tijuana. But believe it or not, it has always been the purity and simplicity of Christ that have drawn millions to Him.

Have you ever explored an avid fly-fisherman's tackle box? It's a veritable arsenal of hundreds, if not thousands, of artificial nymphs on hooks of varying sizes and stealth. And like Adam naming the millions of animals and insects, obsessed fly-fishermen have made the task of assigning names into an art. Grey Ghosts, Flashback Pheasant Tails, Wooly Buggers, Soft Hackles, Silicone Smelts, and Brown Olive Caddises top the list. If you'd like to really impress the anglers, mention Black Humpies and Olive Matukas, then throw in Damsel Flies for effect and you'll be inducted into the elite order of fly-fishing.

As cunning as these hip-wader Houdinis are, they don't hold a candle (or rather a fly rod) to the devil when it comes to counterfeiting. Regardless of what you think of Satan, the Bible warns us about him quite often. More than ninety-one times, he is identified as the *Adversary* and *Tempter*. Like names borrowed from a professional wrestling association, he's also called the *Author of Confusion* and the *Master of Deception*.

> Be of sober spirit, be on the alert. Your adversary, the devil, prowls around like a roaring lion, seeking someone to devour.
>
> 1 Peter 5:8

The biggest surprise of all is that his devious tackle box contains several hooks with your name engraved on them . . . and mine too.

And the shrewd serpent's favorite nymph? You'd think it would be the Grey Ghosts or maybe the Damsel Flies . . . those can catch you off guard!

It has always been the purity and simplicity of Christ that have drawn millions to Him.

They are close, but they do not catch you off guard as effectively as his most devious choice. The devil's favorite jig works best just slightly off the main current, inches left of the chief aim, and a touch off parallel to what's biblical.

It is the lure of a *complicated devotion*.

This myth tries to convince us that staying devoted to Christ is so complicated that most people can only sustain it for two weeks following a church camp. Walking closely to Him requires a monastic regimen that involves a stoic, fun-less life and unflinching dedication to weekly Bible studies and church activities. Following all the rules defines the committed.

It's easy to confuse self-worth with net worth or our spiritual vitality with our spiritual activity. We rate our maturity by what we do:

- How often we go to church
- How many Bible studies we attend each week

- How many times we've read the Bible
- How much we volunteer at church

We become vulnerable to the enemy's distractions when we use the wrong measuring stick. We rate ourselves by what we do rather than who He is. We measure our worth by how many are following what we say and do on Twitter or Facebook rather than how close we are following what Jesus is saying and doing.

> The strength of a man consists in finding out the way in which God is going and going in that way, too.
>
> Henry Ward Beecher

Paul the apostle, however, offers a stark contrast to this line of thinking. The man whom God chose to pen half the New Testament reduced it down to this injunction: *Don't let the devil lead you astray from what is pure and simple about walking with Jesus* (see 2 Corinthians 11:3). In other words, anything about my relationship with God that is less than pure and simple could lead me astray to side currents where troubles stir.

Jesus did not come to complicate the gospel; He came to simplify it without compromising its purity. In times past, religious teachers, in order to retain control, took God just out of the reach of everyday people. A study of church history will reveal whole eras in which the Bible was unavailable to the common citizen. The reason? The leaders of the church were convinced that the average follower could not understand the Scriptures without the "knowledgeables" interpreting them.

It's time to get back to Jesus.

Missing the Real Thing

Have you ever visited the holy sites in Israel? I have been there many times, as I have led several tour groups there over the years. First-timers arrive at the birthplace of Christ, the tomb, or any of the multiple locations that are attached to an event in the life of Christ filled with anticipation and excitement. The pilgrim who arrives anticipating the original setting finds something quite the opposite.

They see hanging incense holders, drapery, regalia, and stained walls covered with soot and artwork. Then there are candles, candles, and more candles—until the original is completely obscured. They take pictures of the accoutrements and hangings, the numerous icons and the overgrowth from centuries of veneration, but they miss the real thing.

We can do the same.

Our dresser drawers are filled with Christian T-shirts, our shelves are lined with spiritual books, and our bling consists of crosses in various sizes and colors. But we can never mistake these for the real thing, a pure and simple closeness with Jesus. My prayer is that when people see you, they will quickly ascertain that you and Jesus hang out together—a lot.

Unfolded Lives

Let's look again at the 2 Corinthians 11:3 passage. The word that Paul used for "simplicity" is *haplotes*. It is an illustrative word that can mean "open" or "unfolded." The word picture is taken from that era's tapestry weavers. Endless yards of colored thread in the hands of craftsmen produced patterns and pictures prized by many. Some merchants would package the artwork with the murals showing, while the remaining parts would be folded and sealed. It was a gift set of sorts neatly framed in a box, ready for purchase and travel.

Other merchants would display the complete hanging. It was presented, without packaging, open and unfolded. The consumer was free to inspect the complete textile with its goodness and flaws together.

> Search me, O God, and know my heart;
> Try me and know my anxious thoughts.
>
> Psalm 139:23

Of course, the packaged artwork was convenient and suitable for immediate shipping. However, cautious buyers shied away from purchasing them, even though merchants assured them of its quality. Most would rather invest in the unfolded hanging than risk the unknown.

A relationship is not sustained by perfection as much as it is by *openness* and *honesty*. Openness is having a heart that allows God to point out where we are drifting. It is a willingness to correct the drift, all the while knowing that His love has not diminished for us in the least. There is nothing that I can do to get Him to love me more, and nothing I can do that will cause Him to love me less.

There is nothing I can do that will cause Him to love me less.

Our desire in this book is to return to Jesus, to ratchet back all the way, to see Him as He really is. In order to accomplish that, we must be ready to live *unfolded* lives.

How open are you in your relationship with Jesus?

Prerequisites to Openness

A generous helping of humility is required to face your own weaknesses. You cannot say that you seek God without seeking the truth. You seldom find something you are not looking for.

He calls us to live life with all the lights on and the windows open. The shadows will sooner or later be dispelled by His radiance and light. First John 1:7 reminds us:

If we walk in the Light as He Himself is in the Light, we have fellowship with one another, and the blood of Jesus His Son cleanses us from all sin.

God's hand and presence refuse to dwell in the shadows. But when we are willing to throw open the curtains to trust Him by doing things His way, our fellowship returns, with Jesus and with others. It's easy to lose confidence when we slip into the shadows. Light becomes intimidating and we are afraid that it will expose our humanity and disqualify our efforts. Living unfolded lives allows His light to wash us on a daily basis.

The Dark Side of Light

For you were formerly darkness, but now you are Light in the Lord; walk as children of Light. . . . Everything that becomes visible is light.

Ephesians 5:8, 13

Light is something we must steward well. When misused, even something that is designed to be good can destroy. Like the Pharisees of old, the mishandling of Scripture has mangled many futures and depleted the potential of untold people's lives.

By the way, Pharisees are still alive and well.

In the first century, they could easily be identified by their clothing and habits. Ringlet sideburns danced as they walked, and their long robes and lofty prayers identified them as the religious elite.

But today Pharisees are far more subtle. They dress and act just like you and me. They work in your workplace and attend your school. They show up in your leadership and volunteer teams. They attend your church!

Surprise.

Modern-day Pharisees work hard at following the rules and creeds. They put great effort into being right, but being right isn't wrong. It is how they steward their being right that is wrong. These phrases seem like tongue twisters, but you are never closer to being completely wrong as when you are convinced that you are right.

Ever met a person like that? So unequivocally certain that they are in the right that every other consideration is thrown to the wind. Anger is now justified. So is disrespect. Slander and accusations are now truth and proclamation. Avenging something that is wrong gives them the right to be harsh and berating.

The religious leaders in Jesus' day were confident that they were right. They were convinced that Jesus was a rebel bent on stirring the crowds. Their sense of rightness made hatred, slander, deception, disrespect, and finally murder, acceptable.

The Messiah, the Redeemer of mankind, was impaled on Golgotha because religious leaders of that day were convinced they were right. Feeling that you are always in the right tends toward your being judgmental. We become the judge, and our justice is always warranted.

> "The Pharisees are not all dead yet, and are not all Jews."
> John McClintock

The Pharisees who were with Him heard these things and said to Him, "We are not blind too, are we?" Jesus said to them, "If you were blind, you would have no sin; but since you say, 'We see,' your sin remains."

John 9:40–41

Being right doesn't give us the right to denounce in judgment. It instead gives us the authority to impart mercy. It puts us in a position to bring wholeness, to overlook an offense or begin restoration.

"There is only one Lawgiver and Judge, the One who is able to save and to destroy" (James 4:12).

Let's correct back to Jesus.

19

Drawing Lines and Building Bridges

Jesus knew when to draw lines and when to build bridges. He leaves us this example to follow.

A group of religious leaders cast a disheveled woman caught in adultery at Jesus' feet. They wanted to test Him. The Hebrew law of Leviticus called for the adulteress to be stoned.

> **In each of us is a Pharisee just waiting to grow up.**

Jesus knew when to draw lines and when to build bridges. He drew a line in the sand to distinguish between the two. He endorsed the Law's demands, but called for only the ones without sin to fulfill the requirements of justice.

One by one, the leaders receded.

With the woman, Jesus built a bridge . . . a bridge to hope and forgiveness.

> He said to her, "Woman, where are those accusers of yours? Has no one condemned you?"
> She said, "No one, Lord."
> And Jesus said to her, "Neither do I condemn you; go and sin no more."
>
> John 8:10–11

Jesus does not compromise when it comes to sin, but He always gives the penitent a way back home.

When you draw close to Him, you will know when to *draw lines* and when to *build bridges*. Ignore this, and you will draw a line where you should have built a bridge, or you will build a bridge where you should have drawn a line.

The religious leaders had the woman all but stoned to death at this point, and bets are that they would have walked away feeling quite holy about the whole ordeal.

In each of us is a Pharisee just waiting to grow up.

An early symptom of self-righteousness surfaces when we begin to judge others based on their actions and ourselves based on our intentions. A second symptom is when we are confident that God dislikes the same people we do!

When you notice these two symptoms, it's time to get back to Jesus.

Questions for individual reflection or group discussion

1. Reread 2 Corinthians 11:3. What things can lead a mind astray from *"the simplicity and purity of devotion to Christ"*?

2. "The devil's favorite jig works best just slightly off the main current, inches left of the chief aim, and a touch just off parallel to what's biblical." Describe some examples you've seen of this when people are so close and yet so far away.

3. Modern-day Pharisees work hard at following spiritual rules and creeds. Without naming names or organizations, how have you seen this in practice?

4. When we draw close to Christ, what benefits result?

CHAPTER 2

JUST SHY OF JESUS

The scribes and the Pharisees brought a woman caught in adultery, and having set her in the center of the court, they said to Him, "Teacher, this woman has been caught in adultery, in the very act."

John 8:3–4

I once attended a camp meeting sponsored by a local evangelist. A group of fifty, mostly Christians, huddled under an expansive white tent with bare lightbulbs hanging from wires strung under its dome. The evangelist's hair was slicked back and his vocal inflections were timed with mechanical gestures. Leaning toward us, his voice boomed over the microphone. The setting made me feel like I was taking part in the filming of a documentary on a revival of the past.

I engaged in a conversation with him later. In the midst of our dialogue, he boldly blurted, "I believe that Jonathan Edwards was the greatest preacher of all time. Only he had the guts to

23

speak the truth without hesitation. As a result, thousands came to Christ."

His bold statement about this fiery evangelist from the 1700s surprised me. I surmised that witnessing the drift of the modern church from her original mission, he corrected back to his hero from Massachusetts. This era fascinated him, and the great evangelist Jonathan Edwards emboldened his methods.

> **Follow not only the teachings of Christ, but also the spirit in which He carried out His teaching.**

I did not doubt the accuracy of his research, but it seemed that the few Christians huddled under the canopy were a far cry from what took place more than 250 years ago. I would admit there needed to be a correction in the church toward evangelism, but if he was going to complete his mission, he'd need to ratchet back a few more years.

All the way back to Jesus.

Not to Prohibition. Not to Wesley or the Great Awakening. Not just to the Reformation or Calvin. Not even to the early church fathers.

All the way back to Jesus.

I am not talking about wearing a robe held in place by a rope. I am talking about following not only the teachings of Christ but also the spirit in which He carried out His teaching.

You cannot stop short.

Coming Up Short

It's easy to come up short and correct back to an era marked by a revival or an awakening. Although we can learn from these inspirational times, they will be incomplete in themselves.

We moved to Oregon during my junior high years after my father, freshly retired from his career in the army, bought ten acres along the Rogue River. It was raw land studded with majestic fir trees and a sparkling creek that ran with spawning salmon. We needed to demarcate our property lines from our neighbor's, so my father decided we needed to build a fence around the area that contained our house and gardens.

I knew that building a fence would require long days and low pay for the junior-high son of a master sergeant. My dad would do the cementing of the posts and hammering of the slats. My job was to cut spacing pieces that would go between boards. My dad instructed me in how to cut an 8-foot 2x4 into 4-inch sections that would be used to space the slats running vertically.

"Measure the first four-inch section and cut it," he instructed. "After you cut one piece, you can save time by using the cut piece to measure the others. I need two hundred of them."

"ALWAYS go back to the original. If you don't, you'll slowly go off."

Sounded easy enough for me, so I started. I measured the first one, cut it, then setting the piece on the 2×4, I scribed it with my pencil, threw the piece on the ground, and cut the second. I then took the cut piece, scribed with it, threw the second piece into the newly formed pile, and cut the third. I repeated this pattern faithfully with only one glitch. You might be able to surmise something I had no clue about at the time: With each fresh cut, the 4-inch piece would grow the width of the pencil mark. Instead of using the original piece, I used the most recently cut one. Over the next fifty or so, it grew incrementally from 4 inches to 4¼ then to 4½ inches. By the hundredth, we were up to 4¾ per piece.

Every so often, my dad would come and grab a handful and use them as spacers. But after an hour, I heard him yelling at me. I turned to see a fence growing in spaces between the uprights. I have to admit, it looked pretty funny. But for some reason, it didn't seem funny to my military dad. He stormed in my direction and asked me what in the world I was doing! I sheepishly showed him what I had been doing and he quickly recognized the problem.

"You always measure with the original cut. ALWAYS go back to the original. If you don't, you'll slowly go off."

For the next four hours, my new assignment was to dismantle the fence so we could replace the spacers. My dad took it upon himself to recut all the spacers.

If he really wanted to cut the spacers himself, why didn't he do it in the first place?!

The Danger of Being One Inch Off

An old theorem states that if your basic premise is inaccurate, every subsequent conclusion you come to will be inaccurate. Astronomers say that if you launch a missile toward Mars and you are one inch off at the launch pad, you will miss Mars by 900 miles. We cannot afford to be even a little off when it comes to Jesus, because even a little shy can be dangerous.

Think about it this way. Plenty of people today have embraced religion, and within that religion they embrace God or Jesus, at least by name. Yet those same "religious" people do not act anywhere near how Jesus acted. It started off well, but slowly, we stopped correcting back to Jesus.

History shows that many religious folk may have started off with good intentions, but they have become some of the biggest perpetrators of chaos and fighting. I'll bet even the Hatfields and McCoys went to church. Remember that most members of the Mafia are known to go to mass on Sunday and shoot you on Monday.

The Crusades, many wars, slavery, and other atrocities all came under the banner of religion.

Adolf Hitler, perhaps the most evil man of the modern era, called himself a Catholic.[1] He bragged about his belief in God. He convinced the masses he was helping the plan of God by ridding the world of Christ's crucifiers.

Whenever you can spiritualize jealousy, pride, or hate, you become a dangerous person, especially when you're a leader of influence. Hitler's faith contained just enough truth to make him dangerous. He corrected back to the Crusades, but not to the original Redeemer, and consequently missed God's best by 900 miles.

> **It's hugely dangerous to be religious without constantly correcting back to Jesus.**

Similarly, another cult leader, David Koresh, believed he was a prophet and lived with his followers on a private compound in Waco, Texas. His Branch Davidian complex was put under siege by the FBI, which finally resulted in the deaths of more than seventy people.

Many Jews and Palestinians of today are very religious people. They worship God, yet they can somehow justify their intense hatred for one another for more than two millennia.

Muslim extremists believe that Allah has ordered the annihilation of infidels. Their beliefs assuage their consciences after committing violent acts of Jihad, leaving thousands dead.

All of these examples point to the same truth: It's hugely dangerous to be religious without constantly correcting back to Jesus.

It's time to get back to Jesus.

Signs of End Times

Is all this a sign of the times? Is it symptomatic of the age of the Antichrist?

1. John Toland, *Adolf Hitler: The Definitive Biography* (New York: Doubleday, 1976), 703.

Believe it or not, three of the numbers on my pickup truck's license plate are 6-6-6. I have had to endure a barrage of constant ribbing for that. I have been identified by the worst of my friends as the Antichrist and by my former friends as the "Beast of the End Times."

I intend to apply for a new license plate soon that boldly states: "I-M-Not."

A concern about end times is nothing new. As far back as the first century AD, people have been looking for clues that identify the Antichrist. Some labeled Nero as a possible candidate. Then in the fifth century, the Antichrist was thought to be the Merovingian dynasty of kings that ruled Europe. Next in line were Hitler, Stalin, the Ayatollah Khomeini, Sun Myung Moon, and Yasser Arafat.[2]

As a piece of trivia, honorable mentions include Bill Gates and former president Bill Clinton.[3]

For years, the Antichrist has been thought to be one person. He may well be exactly that, but I'm considering another option.

Let's take a closer look at a passage in Revelation:

> Here is wisdom. Let him who has understanding calculate the number of the beast, for the number is that of man; and his number is six hundred and sixty-six.
>
> Revelation 13:18

This Scripture has always intrigued me to no end.

Revelation is a cryptic book to begin with, and what makes it even tougher to understand is that the stories are not necessarily written in chronological order. It bounces between Mary protecting her child in Matthew to the fall of Lucifer in Ezekiel. Then it fast-forwards to the end days, prophets, and the tribulation, then back to the church and her apostasy.

---

2. Todd Strandberg, "The Antichrist: Have You Seen This Man?" www.raptureready.com/rr-antichrist.html.

3. Ibid.

Just Shy of Jesus

To consider a plausible interpretation of the text, first calculate the perfect number of God. Rabbis and students of biblical code often say that God's number is seven and the numbers 7-7-7 would be the perfect number for the Trinity—one God in three persons.

If we take God's number as 7-7-7, then it would make sense that the number assigned to people would be slightly below God's. People, who are made in God's image, are capable of being redeemed and receiving eternal life; we have the capacity to host the living Holy Spirit within our spirits. This is who God created to be in His image and to be couriers of the message of salvation.

I believe there is indeed one Beast who factors into the end times (ultimately Lucifer), but the spirit of the antichrist may rest in the number of all of mankind still living, men and women who are just shy of God's best.

The Greek word *apostasy* comes from two words: one means *away from,* and the other means the *stance* that you take. You can't have a falling away from something if there were not first *a standing for something.* So the apostasy in the last days may well be Christians or people representing Christ who have broken away or fallen away from the stance we once took.

Those 666-ers may very well be those people who are just shy of God's best, just short of 777. It will not be those far from the image of God's best—not the 222s or 333s. History records that the ones who have done great damage are the religiously mis-inclined. These are the ones who can define God. They can give the correct answers about God. They even know about God, but stop just shy of an authentic relationship with Jesus Christ.

They know enough to soothe their consciences and justify their actions. Revelation 3:15–16 states, "I wish that you were cold or hot. So because you are lukewarm, and neither hot nor cold, I will spit you out of My mouth."

We've all witnessed this. It's not the Wiccans, anarchists, or even atheists who raise the greatest doubts about Jesus. Rather, it is the religious who espouse unbiblical actions and clothe them with Scripture: modern-day Pharisees, twenty-first-century gnostics, and seminary-graduate scribes.

> Correct all the way back to Jesus. . . . Anything shorter and you will end up a modern-day Pharisee.

The devil may be defeated, but he is not stupid. He is very crafty. His plan has always been to recruit 666s to carry out his bidding: false prophets, religious leaders, and crusaders. These may be those among our ranks who have enough truth to convince people and enough deception to conflict them.

Fishermen say the temptation that catches fish is usually 99 percent good-tasting bait . . .

And 1 percent hook.

Satan knows he cannot convince people while wearing a red suit and brandishing a pitchfork. However, he also knows that if he can camouflage his 1 percent deception with 99 percent truth, he can net a bunch of fish!

> Even Satan disguises himself as an angel of light. Therefore it is not surprising if his servants also disguise themselves as servants of righteousness.
>
> 2 Corinthians 11:14–15

The solution is to correct all the way back to Jesus, to His teachings and to the spirit in which He taught. Anything short of that and you will end up a modern-day Pharisee. But Pharisees aren't made just on the short side. They make great ones on the long side too.

Let me explain.

Don't Overshoot

The devil does not care which side of the boat you go off, so long as you go off.

Another mistake we make is not coming up on the short end, but overshooting Christ. In fear of coming up short, we go beyond what is written—just for "insurance." We hold others to a standard that disqualifies most of the earth's population. It is a regimen for only an elite club (of which we are charter members).

The Pharisees did that. They'd define and apply the Scriptures in an overly stringent fashion to ensure that people did not fall prey to sin. For instance, in fear of violating the Sabbath, the rabbis mandated that Jews not leave their homes for a twenty-four-hour period. Or to ensure that no one would look upon a woman with lust, husbands would cover their wives in public until they resembled walking drapes.

We might chuckle at the overkill, but we do the same thing today. Of course, it is much more civilized and "theologically astute."

We hold endless debates about Christians who drink, see R-rated movies, or take part in dancing, smoking, or other tobacco usage. We evaluate each other's behavior and activities as if our spiritual gift is to hold court sessions about the true maturity of other believers.

But is that really what Jesus wants us to do? So much energy is expended judging one another. Really, much of this judging is tantamount to shoving people around in the name of religion.

It's time to get back to Jesus.

A First-Class Bother

A few years ago I was flying back to Hawaii after a week in Australia. I fly often, so I have a quiver full of airline miles that automatically bumps me up to business or first class, should seats be available. I was returning home after an intense week of teaching in Perth, where more than 12,000 people attended an open-air crusade. When I arrived at the airport, I was thrilled to notice that I was bumped up to first class. After all, I was dog-tired and ready for a long winter's nap. I was just settling in when a man walked up the aisle and nudged me out of my slumber.

"Aren't you Wayne Cordeiro, the pastor who has a television program?"

"Yes," I replied. "How are you tonight?"

Without answering my question, the man launched into his sermon.

"I thought you are supposed to be a Christian example," he said. "If you really are, you should have given up your first-class seat to someone else and gotten in the back. That's what Jesus would have done."

I thought that if Jesus were sitting here as tired as I was, He might have called this bother a viper or something more descriptive.

But I refrained.

I'm sure this man knew Jesus, but he overshot Him. He held me to an implausible standard that he himself was not able to maintain. (He was a businessman flying first class as well.)

Instead, I simply said, "Excuse me, but I am really tired. Can I just go to sleep now? You might find it beneficial to do the same. Good night."

Paul recognized the tendency of people who overshoot Jesus. He addressed it in his letter to the churches in Corinth:

> Learn not to exceed what is written, so that no one of you will become arrogant in behalf of one against the other.
>
> 1 Corinthians 4:6

Overrunning Jesus can make us feel superior and be deluded into thinking we are the only true believers on our planet.

It's time to get back to Jesus.

Questions for individual reflection or group discussion

1. In the first part of this chapter, we read these words: "Sometimes you are never more wrong than when you are convinced that you are right." What do you think that means? Have you witnessed this in your life?

2. What is a modern-day Pharisee? How have you seen people using Scripture in an overly stringent manner that ends up hurting people?

3. Discuss what 1 Corinthians 4:6 means: "Learn not to exceed what is written, so that no one of you will become arrogant in behalf of one against the other."

4. During the last days, Satan may recruit a multitude of "religious" people to do his bidding. Could we be our greatest obstacle? Discuss this possibility.

CHAPTER 3

AVOIDING THE SUBCULTURE

His mother said to Him, "Son, why have You treated us this way? Behold, Your father and I have been anxiously looking for You." And He said to them, "Why is it that you were looking for Me? Did you not know that I had to be in My Father's house?"

Luke 2:48–49

There is an old fable that contains a great measure of truth.

A farmer had a small home-grown business making grease for his tractor and farm equipment. He was dissatisfied with the quality he found in the local hardware stores, so he began experimenting with his own concoctions and eventually came up with a winner.

Soon the farmer's neighbors began requesting his grease because of its superior quality. These requests compelled him to increase the size of his weekend project, and soon he invested in sufficient equipment for a small manufacturing business.

Eventually the farmer's sales increased to the point that he decided to stop farming and make grease full time. He hired employees, and soon his manufacturing plant was shipping barrels of grease to locations around the world.

The farmer tore down his farm buildings and constructed a large manufacturing plant on the site. His grease machines increased from a few to thousands of moving parts to keep up with the orders that poured in each day.

Then something happened that no one noticed at first. Much of the grease the farmer manufactured had to be withheld to lubricate the thousands of moving parts in his manufacturing plant. Over the years, imperceptibly, his own factory grew, and with it grew costs and the need for maintenance, grease, and employees. Soon the day came when the grease plant could not fulfill orders and went bankrupt. The reason?

All the grease it was producing had to be used to grease its own machines. Everything they produced was used on their own equipment.

That reminds me of our modern-day denominations and churches. We use everything we produce to maintain ourselves!

We received a God-given assignment to take His heart to the world. Instead, we have built a Christian subculture. We now have our own music, our own fashions, movies, and concerts. We have our own credit unions, our own diet programs, and even our own Scripture mints (because surely Christians should have fresher breath than non-Christians)!

Now, there's nothing inherently wrong with any of this. I partake in many of these myself! But we have forgotten who we are and what we are doing here.

I tell a story in the book *Doing Church as a Team*. A discouraged rabbi in the Siberian tundra wandered from his home. Disenchanted with his ministry and life, he aimlessly ambled into the wintry night. The only thing that was colder than the evening air was the chill in his own soul. He was so discouraged that he aimlessly wandered by mistake into a nearby Russian military compound that was off limits to any civilian personnel.

The only sound was the crunch of the freshly fallen snow under his boots, when the evening still was broken by the brash bark of a Russian soldier brandishing a rifle.

> We have forgotten who we are and what we are doing here.

"Hey!" he shouted, startling the rabbi. "Who are you and what are you doing here?"

The rabbi thought for a moment and looked up. "How much do they pay you each day?" he asked innocently.

"What does that have to do with this?" the soldier growled back.

The rabbi said, "I will pay you the same sum if you will ask me that question every morning: *Who are you and what are you doing here?*"

Let me be that Russian soldier for you in this chapter and ask you: *Who are you and what are you doing here?*

It's time to examine the way we live, to throw off the yoke of Christian subculture and get back to Jesus.

Don't Forget

Not much detail is disclosed in the Gospels concerning Jesus' early life. In the opening scenes, we find Him at age twelve in Jerusalem. Families from Nazareth in Galilee traveled in caravans to attend the annual Passover festivities. It was safer that way, and it gave the cousins company and playmates on the journey.

In Jerusalem, families looked forward to the sacrifices and feasting, which allowed for the renewing of old acquaintances. But now it was time to make the long trip homeward. They struck their tents, pulled up stakes, and headed north. Thinking that Jesus was with a cousin in a relative's wagon, Mary and Joseph proceeded up the dusty road to Nazareth. What they did not know was that Jesus had remained behind.

"Your career is what you're paid for. Your calling is what you're made for."

But His parents were unaware of it . . . and they began looking for Him among their relatives and acquaintances. When they did not find Him, they returned to Jerusalem looking for Him.

Luke 2:43–45

They launched a three-day search, and each morning brought a rising anxiety to Mary's heart. On the third day, someone informed her of a young man in the temple who was stumping the elders, so she quickly turned her search in the direction of the local synagogue. The informant was correct. Seeing Him sitting with the Pharisees and religious leaders, Mary approached Jesus with relief mixed with emotion:

Son, why have You done this to us? Look, your father and I have sought you anxiously.

With an uncanny calmness not usually found in preadolescents, He replied:

Why did you seek Me? Did you not know that I must be about My Father's business?

Luke 2:48–49 NKJV

Jesus knew His assignment early on. He knew His calling; He had to be about His Father's business. It transcended everything else: His carpentry, His friendships, even His parents' expectations.

It's easy to get our callings mixed up with our careers. The latter often overshadows the former, and for some, it can take a lifetime to balance out. I recall hearing an old saying that still holds true today: "Your career is what you're paid for. Your calling is what you're made for." Forgetting who we are or measuring who we are with wrong metrics will cause us to lose not only our purpose but also our identity. Israel kept forgetting who she was until she blended into the culture that surrounded her.

As Christ-followers, we can easily end up being what I call "Christian chameleons"—we blend into whatever background we happen to be a part of, and it camouflages who we really are. We all fight the tendency to get sucked into the vortex of the world. Eloquent pastors trade in their callings for career paths that will lead to a greater following. A question I must always ask myself is, "When all is said and done, will they see more of Jesus or more of me?"

Rather than our careers, families, athletic teams, clubs, or hobbies, we must primarily be about our Father's interests while on this earth.

- As a father, you are not first a disciplinarian. You are a discipler.
- Mom, your main role is not to make meals, but to make disciples.
- As a student, your first concern is not to be popular or admired. It is to be an example of the heart of Christ regardless of your approval ratings.

Oswald Chambers said, "When you fear God, you fear nothing else, whereas if you do not fear God, you fear everything else."

I always wondered, if Jesus walked physically among us today—wearing jeans instead of a robe—how long would it take for others to recognize that He was different? If He worked in our offices or attended our schools, what would be the length of time before people recognized something special about Him?

One month? Two months? A year?

How long does it take people in your environment to recognize that you walk with Jesus and that you are identified with eternity?

One month? Two months? A year? Never?

- Getting back to Jesus means remembering who you are and being OK with that.
- Getting back to Jesus means being satisfied with who God made you to be regardless of how you stack up with the world.
- Getting back to Jesus means taking your joy from what God is doing in you rather than from what you are doing for Him.
- Getting back to Jesus means staying with what is pure and simple—pure and simple.

Another World

One of my favorite quotes is from John Wesley, who said, "I judge all things only by the price they shall gain in eternity."

Jesus consistently reminded His disciples of the fact that another world awaits. Our world now is the field of our assignment, not our permanent home. When the temple guards came to arrest Jesus, Peter drew a sword to protect the unarmed teacher and to level the playing field. But the Lord said,

> Put your sword in its place, for all who take the sword will perish by the sword. Or do you think that I cannot now pray

to My Father, and He will provide Me with more than twelve legions of angels?

Matthew 26:52–53 NKJV

Later Pilate asked Jesus why He did not defend himself as was common when one was accused falsely. He again reminded us:

My kingdom is not of this world. If My kingdom were of this world, My servants would fight, so that I should not be delivered to the Jews.

John 18:36 NKJV

In the end, the church will not be defined so much by what we separated ourselves from, but by that to which we have given ourselves. Jesus gave His life to reaching lost people for eternity's sake.

When I stand before the throne of God, He won't ask me, "How many friends did you have on Facebook?" or "How many hits did you get on your website?"

I personally think He will ask, "How many did you bring with you?"

One of the most important aspects of our lives after becoming a Christian will be the kind of influence we have on others. Each of us will influence someone. It could be good or bad; it could nudge people toward the cross or away from it; it could be positive, negative, or neutral, but we will all influence those we come in contact with in one way or another.

Jesus put it this way: "Neither do people light a lamp and put it under a bowl. Instead, they put it on its stand, and it gives light to everyone in the house. In the same way, let your light shine before others, that they may see your good deeds and glorify your Father in heaven" (Matthew 5:15–16 NIV).

At the very core of our life, our purpose is very simple and very pure:

- Know Jesus intimately.
- Live life accordingly.
- Influence others appropriately.

Of Weeds and Men

It's easy to get sidetracked and fill our lives with what Jesus called "other things" in the parable of the sower and the seed. A life filled with other things resembles a garden that has never been weeded. There are vegetables somewhere all right, but the weeds make it hard to enjoy them, let alone harvest them.

> The worries of this life, the deceitfulness of wealth and the desires for other things come in and choke the word, making it unfruitful.
>
> Mark 4:19 NIV

God will not hold us accountable for how much we have done. He will hold us accountable for how much we have done of what *He has asked us to do*. We cannot forget our assignment. Jesus reminds us that just as He did, we too must somehow never forget that we are to be a counterculture designed "to seek and to save the lost" (Luke 19:10 NIV).

Jesus never asked us to be a subculture.

He asked us to be a counterculture.

Out of the Saltshaker

Jesus said it simply in Matthew 5:13 (NLT):

> You are the salt of the earth. But what good is salt if it has lost its flavor? Can you make it salty again? It will be thrown out and trampled underfoot as worthless.

It is said that within ten years of becoming Christians, most of us no longer have many non-church friends. Of course, on one hand, that can be healthy. Fellowshiping with other Christians is always a positive thing. But on the other hand, if we retreat from those who need Jesus the most, we will miss our mission. It can feel lonely out there, but if the granules of salt collect back in the saltshaker, the entire meal is in trouble. As Rebecca Manley Pippert put it, the goal is to get the salt out of the saltshaker and into the world.[1]

Jesus never said that we would be the majority of the earth. He said we would be the *salt of the earth*.

Thanksgiving has always been a family gathering time for our tribe, and somehow over the years, I have been dubbed the chief cook—for the turkey, at least. With all due respect to Colonel Sanders, I have my own secret herbs and spices. But one of the main ingredients I use is a reddish salt from the island of Kauai called *alaea* salt. I sprinkle it over the turkey (in a certain secret fashion, that is), but it surely is not the majority of the holiday fare. The sparse granules are hardly recognizable.

In comparison to the fifteen-pound turkey, the salt is definitely in the minority; however, it influences the savor of the whole.

Jesus did not say the war would be lost by the side with fewer troops. He said it would be lost if those troops lose their sense of assignment.

If we retreat from those who need Jesus the most, we will miss our mission.

Go, Therefore . . .

So how do we break out of the subculture without abandoning our safe havens of fellowship? How can we be *in* this world without becoming one *of* this world?

1. Rebecca Manley Pippert, *Out of the Saltshaker and Into the World* (Downers Grove, IL: InterVarsity Press, 1979).

The answer can be found in the Great Commission. Matthew 28:18–20 (NKJV) reads:

> Jesus came and spoke to them, saying, "All authority has been given to Me in heaven and on earth. Go therefore and make disciples of all the nations, baptizing them in the name of the Father and of the Son and of the Holy Spirit, teaching them to observe all things that I have commanded you; and lo, I am with you always, even to the end of the age."

Any precision instrument, such as a camera or microscope, a micrometer or automobile engine, needs to be periodically recalculated. You don't tune the engine once and leave it alone. Just by reason of use, it will require recalibrations and tune-ups. A technician will reset it to factory specifications or preset requirements for optimum performance.

In like manner, Jesus gives us the Great Commission to re-calibrate the steadiness of our souls in a bumpy world. We are easily shaken from our heavenly composure and we lose our way on uneven paths. God's design is for us to recalibrate our direction with the compass of His Word so we won't be found in the category of *Once I was found . . . but now I am lost.*

In His Image

His goal for us is not leisure. It is *likeness.*

> For whom He foreknew, He also predestined to be conformed to the image of His Son.
>
> Romans 8:29 NKJV

God created you to be molded in such a way that your life coincides with His Son's. That was His original purpose and it is still His unprecedented goal. The more you press in to Jesus, the more you become the person God created you to be.

In other words, the more you become like Jesus, the more you become yourself!

But it won't be a cakewalk. Being like Jesus will exact a price. It will demand the death of our fleshly desire to be conformed to the world. Our natural tendency is to allow the cravings of our human nature to trump the desires of the Spirit of God for us.

Some months ago I had the privilege of speaking to a group of college students on this topic. One stood up and said, "Are you saying that we should have no desires at all? That would not even be plausible! As a young man, what do I do with all my desires?"

My answer was simply this: "I am not asking you to get rid of all your desires. Instead, make your greatest desire to serve Jesus Christ. When He is your greatest and deepest desire, your other desires will fall into their proper places."

> **His goal for us is not leisure. It is *likeness*.**

A Costly Treasure

No matter how long you have been a Christian and a follower of Christ, your flesh is still alive and well, and if given the slightest chance, it will take the reins. The flesh can take on a cloak of transparency and even spirituality, but it lurks underneath, searching for ways to express itself. I remember a pastor once saying, "Salvation is free, but everything else costs."

I didn't understand it at that time, but over the years his words began to ring clear and true.

- If you want a healthy marriage, it will cost you something.
- If you want a strong faith, it will cost you time, effort, and self-discipline.

- If you want a wise heart, it will cost you your ego and pride.
- If you want to be like Jesus, it will cost you everything.

But the return is gargantuan. It is like a man who found a treasure worth millions in a field and, over the joy of finding it, sold everything he had in order to buy that field. He knew that the value of the hidden fortune would be worth far more than what he had in his bank account or all the possessions he had stored in his closets and garage. (See Matthew 13:44.)

Jesus is where we will find our greatest value, and sometimes the Lord will nudge us to get rid of unnecessary baggage: time-consuming behaviors, self-defeating perceptions, relationship-destroying attitudes, and greed-building habits.

As you fully give yourself to being a person of the kingdom, everything begins to shift.

- The way you spend money expresses how much you treasure Jesus, not how much you treasure wealth.
- The way you run your business expresses how much you treasure Jesus, not how much you treasure profit.
- The way you treat people reflects how much you treasure Jesus, not how much you treasure admiration from others.

Let Jesus Wash You

God made us in His image, but as we go along, we often pick up habits and patterns of the world like lint on a dark wool coat. It's neither deliberate nor premeditated. It simply gathers along the way, and if we ignore this natural accumulation, we will find ourselves in a slow drift to becoming someone we never wanted to be.

In John 13, Jesus came to Peter to wash his feet, and when the disciple realized what Jesus was about to do, his self-sufficiency spoke out: "You don't need to wash my feet!" Jesus answered and said, "If I don't wash your feet, you'll have no part of Me." In other words, Jesus was saying, "If you don't let Me wash your feet, we can't be close." Peter must have caught it because he immediately replied, "If that's the case, then give me a bath!" Jesus must have smiled and said to him that he just needed to cleanse the dust of the Jerusalem streets from his feet. By simply traversing the corridors of the ancient city, the dust that clung to his feet needed to be washed off. (See vv. 5–10.)

As Christians, we are each still a part of humanity, and as we navigate through this spinning earth, we too will have the world's dust clinging to our words, habits, thoughts, and attitudes.

Jesus will often come by to wash us.

Why?

So we can be close again.

Remember: *Do not be afraid to let Him remove from you what you are not, lest you become what you never wanted to be.*

God's Persistent Process

The story is told of Michelangelo finishing his greater-than-life-size marble sculpture of David. Scattered about the sculpture was a layer of marble dust and chips. An admiring bystander who had been watching the image of David emerge from the stone finally asked, "How are you able to create such an amazing figure from just a block of marble!?"

"Easy," the master replied. "I really don't create David. He's already in there. I simply chip away everything that isn't David!"

It's time to chip back to Jesus.

As the deer pants for the water brooks, so my soul pants for You, O God. My soul thirsts for God, for the living God.

Psalm 42:1–2

Questions for individual reflection or group discussion:

1. This chapter opens with a parable of a manufacturing plant that eventually comes to exist only for itself. What's the meaning of this parable when it comes to the way we live?

2. Reread Luke 2:48–49. Jesus knew His assignment early on. What was it, and what does it mean for us to similarly be about our Father's business?

3. A question was posed in this chapter: "How long does it take people in your environment to recognize that you walk with Jesus and that you are identified with eternity?" How would you answer this?

4. How do we have the tendency to build a subculture rather than be a counterculture? What are some practical ways to remember that our goal is to reach the world, not run from it?

5. What can be the risks to being in the world without becoming one with the world?

6. Discuss what this sentence might mean: "Salvation is free. Everything else costs."

CHAPTER 4

WHO IS THIS JESUS?

He is the image of the invisible God.

Colossians 1:15

Take a moment and think only about Jesus.

Think through the stories you know of Him, what He's like, what He's said, and what He's done.

Picture His humble beginnings in Bethlehem—lying in swaddling clothes in a manger bed, Mary and Joseph close by.

See Him as a young boy in the temple, growing in favor with God and men.

See Him at age thirty, being baptized in the Jordan River by John the Baptist. The Spirit of God descending on Jesus in the form of a dove and a voice calling from heaven, "This is my Son, whom I love; with him I am well pleased" (Matthew 3:17 NIV).

See Jesus in the wilderness, resisting temptation. He never waivers from His purpose. He stands tall against Satan, and returns to Galilee in the power of the Spirit (Luke 4:14).

See Jesus calling His first disciples. They are simple, ordinary, unschooled fishermen. These unlikely candidates will one day change the world.

See Jesus teaching the Beatitudes. He's up on a mountainside, and the crowds have gathered around Him. They're eager to hear about this man who talks about such strange new ideas. *Blessed are the poor?!* They like the sound of that!

Imagine Jesus healing a man with leprosy, a paralytic, and a man born blind. See Him talking with the woman at the well and eating with tax collectors and sinners. See Him raising Lazarus and a twelve-year-old girl from the dead.

See Jesus walking on water. "Take courage," He says. "Don't be afraid." Even the winds and waves obey Him.

Meet with Him as He feeds huge crowds of people. Then quietly watch with Him as He prays alone early in the morning.

See little children flocking toward Him. Children always know when someone's the real deal.

See Him transfigured high on a mountaintop with His three closest disciples—Peter, James, and John. Jesus is radiant and clothed in dazzling white garments.

Watch Him riding into Jerusalem on the back of a donkey. See Him clearing the temple of the money changers.

See Him washing the feet of His disciples in the upper room.

Observe Him as He is betrayed.

Look at Him hanging on the cross. Listen as He cries out in a loud voice, "It is finished!"

See Him still, cold, lifeless, lying in the tomb.

Hear the deafening silence.

See Him alive again! Walking, talking, eating!

Now He's in the garden. He's asking Mary why she's crying. She turns to Him and suddenly realizes who He is. *"Rabboni!"* she says in Aramaic, which means "Teacher!" (See John 20:16.)

Now He's on a beach after the disciples have fished all night. At first they haven't caught anything, but Jesus has already prepared a fire for the miraculous catch.

See Jesus lifting up His hands, blessing His disciples, and then ascending into heaven.

By thinking these thoughts, meditating on the life of Jesus, do you know what you've just done? You have . . .

> Set your mind on the things above, not on the things that are on earth. For you have died and your life is hidden with Christ in God.
>
> Colossians 3:2–3

Jesus invites us to continually shift our focus onto himself.

It is so important for believers to learn and practice this consistent discipline of setting our hearts and minds on things above. It's far too easy to be consumed by the difficulties and concerns of each day. Yet Jesus invites us to continually shift our focus onto himself, the image of the unseen God (Colossians 1:15). This practice is necessary if we want to enjoy a pure and simple devotion.

But it may not be as easy as it looks.

The Continental Divide

If we want to consistently focus on Jesus, we need to know for certain that the gap between us and God has been bridged.

Are you familiar with this great gap?

Think about big gaps you know.

There is a line that in tectonic terms is called a continental divide. The line determines which way rivers flow.

The continental divide in the Americas is known as the Great Divide. It begins in Alaska, runs down through the Rockies, through Mexico, and into the Andes in South America.

Rivers on the west side of the Great Divide usually flow toward the Pacific Ocean or the Sea of Cortez, and the rivers on the east either flow toward the Atlantic Ocean or the Gulf of Mexico.

Yet the most important divide is not a physical one or even one that separates groups of people. This line runs straight through the hearts of men and women, between them and eternity. It is the invisible gaping rift between God and mankind.

The Bible describes what separates us from God:

The wages of sin is death.

Romans 6:23

The heart of God is to bridge that gap, but He will not force us to walk to the other side of the passageway. When we reject God, we are left to live with the wages.

Death has two definitions.

One is the cessation of life. This is when our lungs refuse to bring in the fresh air that surrounds us. Death shortly follows.

The other definition of death is not a stoppage but a *separation* from life. You still exist, but what is designed to give vibrancy vanishes. You are at the end of your rope and you survive for today with no hope for tomorrow.

This separation from life exists because mankind decided to say no to God and built up a wall that divides us from God. This is the chasm—the Great Divide. We could not reach God because we rejected Him. God in His holiness could have nothing to do with sin.

But there is hope.

But now in Christ Jesus, you who were far away from God are brought near through the blood of Christ's death.

Ephesians 2:13 NCV

We did not reach up to God; God reached down to us. When we are willing to accept God's forgiveness and invitation of real life through Christ, we become the children of God. You receive a new heart, which is a new way of seeing life—not only the ability to see with new eyes, but the power to change your behavior by changing your heart.

> Therefore if anyone is in Christ, he is a new creature; the old things passed away; behold, new things have come.
>
> 2 Corinthians 5:17

The divide has been bridged and now we can cross over. Have you done that?

A Simple but Eternal Question

> Therefore repent and return, so that your sins may be wiped away, in order that times of refreshing may come from the presence of the Lord; and that He may send Jesus, the Christ appointed for you.
>
> Acts 3:19–20

Each of us will have an appointment with God. It will either be here as we walk on this earth or it will be as we stand before Him on that fateful day, but the Holy Spirit will ensure that during our lifetime, each of us will come face-to-face with a decision about Jesus Christ.

I suspect that if you are reading this book, crossing that bridge and coming to Christ is something you've already done. But if you are yet unsure, settle that now and forever, because your forever depends on it.

If you have indeed chosen to walk with Christ, that decision alone does not guarantee your success. Sin pursues each of us without partiality. There are millions of Christians who have eternal life but do not have *abundant life*.

I have come that they may have life, and that they may have it more abundantly.

John 10:10 NKJV

Jesus came to bring us a *quality of life* as well as a quantity of life. My goal in this chapter is to convince you, as strange as it may seem, not to settle for eternal life, the life you will receive on the other side of the line. I challenge you to pursue a quality of living on this side. No, not a leisurely lifestyle of self-absorbed opulence, but rather a life that walks closely with the Author of Life with your whole goal to make Him known!

An angel of the Lord appeared to Joseph in a dream, saying,

She will bear a Son; and you shall call His name Jesus, for *He will save His people from their sins.*

Matthew 1:21 (emphasis added)

Jesus not only came to save the lost from their sins, He also came to save *the found*!

Separation from true life affects Christians as well as non-Christians. Sin must be washed away often and consistently, like the dust that collected on Peter's feet. Our nearness to the Author of Life depends on it.

Often the separation that afflicts Christians comes in far more subtle ways. It comes clothed in religious garb, and it can even begin with innocent motives.

Innocent but immature.

Looking in All the Wrong Places

Sometimes we can get separated from Christ, and finding our way back is difficult because we're looking for Him in the wrong places.

A few years back I was going through a difficult patch at work, so I went to the North Shore of Oahu to spend the whole night on the beach. I wanted to talk to God face-to-face. In prayer I said, "God, I am going to stay here all night because I need a fresh encounter with your glory. I need to experience you with my eyes. Please, let me see you tonight."

I sat on a little chair in the sand and waited. I was certain that I was about to have an epiphany any time now. This would make such a great testimony! It would change my ministry. It would propel me forward with an amazing passion for the lost.

I prayed.

I sang.

I cried.

I confessed.

I walked up and down the beach and I waited. I looked around a tree and thought, "Maybe He's late." I waited the whole night until the dawn began to peek over the eastern hills. Morning arrived and no God! I was frustrated and tired. I thought, "I waited all night and God didn't come. I needed to see Him but I didn't! What will become of me?"

Have you ever done that? Your search may not have consumed a whole night, but I'll bet it consumed your whole thoughts. Have you ever expected, believed, and had faith for something that just didn't happen, leaving you dejected and confused?

- You prayed for the health of a loved one and they died.
- You believed for a job and you didn't get hired.
- You had faith to get married to a certain person, but they didn't have the same faith to marry you.
- You prayed for safety and got injured.

What I discovered later was that I was trying to see Him incorrectly. My physical eyes don't work well when it comes to seeing God. I was depending on sight for proof.

That was my first mistake.

And though you have not seen Him, you love Him, and though you do not see Him now, but believe in Him, you greatly rejoice with joy inexpressible and full of glory.

1 Peter 1:8

Let's make this very practical.

How often have we longed for an encounter with God and yet focused our hearts and minds on our earthly problems rather than divine promises?

For instance, we say things like:

- Lord, I'm in a hard marriage. Why I can't leave this relationship?
- God, I'm broke. I don't know how I am going to make it financially.
- God, I need a job so desperately. Why am I unemployed right now?
- Jesus, my teenage daughter is running wild. She's ruining our home. What can we do?
- God, my parents are elderly and need so much help. But I'm stretched thin right now. How am I ever going to care for them?
- God, I'm thirty-four years old and thought I'd be married by now. Why am I still single?

In those situations, we often do what I did on the beach. We want God to show up on our terms, answer our questions, and prove himself in ways that please us.

But when God does not, we become disappointed, angry, and frustrated. I have learned over the years that the Lord hardly ever gives me an answer.

Instead, He gives me a promise.

Do you know the difference between an *answer* and a *promise*?

- For the single person struggling with loneliness, He gives a promise:

  Lo, I will be with you always, even unto the end of the age.

  Matthew 28:20

- For the person fraught by insufficient finances, God gives a promise:

  Trust in the Lord with all your heart and do not lean on your own understanding. In all your ways acknowledge Him, and He will make your paths straight.

  Proverbs 3:5–6

- For the person stressed and worried about how she's going to care for her elderly parents, God gives a promise:

  I can do all things through Him who strengthens me.

  Philippians 4:13

- For the parents fearful about where their wayward daughter is, worried about whom she is with and what she is doing, God seldom gives an answer. Instead, He gives a promise:

  I will never desert you, nor will I ever forsake you.

  Hebrews 13:5

- For the out-of-work person desperate to get a job, God offers a promise.

  "For I know the plans that I have for you," declares the Lord, "plans for welfare and not for calamity, to give you a future and a hope."

  Jeremiah 29:11

Here now lies the reason for promises over answers:

He has granted to us His precious and magnificent promises, so that by them you may become partakers of the divine nature.

2 Peter 1:4

In other words, God says, "If I answered your question, you wouldn't change, but if you understand my promise, it will make you a partaker of my divine nature." Something happens inside and I see God is bigger than my problems. That's what makes us more like Jesus. Not temporary answers to questions. It is as I understand the promises of God that I learn to trust in His provision and timing. When I catch His promises, then I know how God has been faithful from the beginning of time, not just to me, but to all mankind.

I'm able then to lift my eyes off my problem and set them onto things above.

It is like lifting weights. If you want to build muscle, you start by lifting thirty pounds. But after a while, thirty pounds begins to feel light.

Is it because the weight got lighter?

No! It is because your muscles got stronger.

It's the same with our faith. When God gives us His promises, it builds our faith. He allows our faith to be tested through various trials that put pressure on us. That builds strength. Over time, the same problem that we used to strain and groan under is now for some reason, very light.

We grow in faith.

Testimony From a TB Sanitarium

Something powerful happens when we focus our hearts and minds on things above. We understand the mind of Christ. We realize what matters most to Him, and then we begin to act as Jesus acted. We start to live out the ministry of Christ. It's not always comfortable or tidy. But life becomes a new sort of adventure.

Let me close this chapter with the story of Doug Nichols, founder and international director emeritus of Action International Ministries. In 1967, he was with Operation Mobilization, working in India, when he contracted tuberculosis and was committed to a sanitarium for several months.

In the TB sanitarium, Doug found himself in a lonely, confusing, and troubled place. He did not know the language of the other patients, but he wanted to share the Good News with them—to invite them to focus their hearts and eyes on things above.

All Doug had in the sanitarium were a few gospel tracts in their language, Parsee. He tried to pass them out, but nobody wanted them. They thought he was just another weird American. Doug didn't know what to do. He was sick, in pain, and in the hospital. None of his efforts at sharing the Good News had worked.

Then one night, Doug woke up at 2:00 AM, coughing so violently that he could not catch his breath. During this coughing fit, Doug noticed a little old emaciated man across the aisle trying to get out of bed. He was so weak he could not stand up. He began to whimper. He tried again, but to no avail.

In the morning Doug realized that the man had been trying to get up to use the bathroom. The stench in the ward was terrible. The other patients were angry at the old man for not being able to contain himself. The nurse cleaned up the mess and then slapped the man.

The next night, the very same thing happened. Doug woke up coughing. Again, he saw the old man trying to get out of bed, but he could not stand up, so he began to cry softly and whimper as he rolled back into his bed.

That night, instead of turning over, Doug got out of his bed. In his weakened state he went over to the old man. They didn't speak the same language, but Doug picked him up and carried him to the toilet (just a hole in the floor) and then brought him back to his bed. The old man kissed Doug on the cheek and promptly went to sleep.

Early the next morning, Doug awoke to a steaming cup of tea beside his bed. Another patient had kindly made it for him. The patient motioned that he wanted one of those gospel tracts. The next two days, one after another patient asked, "Could I have one of those tracts too?"

Do you see what happened?

Doug had begun to truly live by this verse:

> Set your minds on things above, not on the things that are on the earth. For you died and your life is hidden with Christ in God.
>
> Colossians 3:2–3

When Doug set his heart and mind on things above, his actions followed. He began not only to know about the ministry of Christ, but to live it before others. Doug's actions proclaimed the excellencies of God, and by his simple act of service people were now convinced that God was with them.[1]

Do you want to see Jesus?

Begin to focus on who He is, on what He did, and on the promises He gives us in His Word. When your heart and mind are set on things above, your actions will follow.

And you will find yourself walking much more closely with the Author of Life.

That's Jesus—pure and simple.

---

1. Doug Nichols, "Witnessing in a TB Sanitarium," Action International Ministries, www.actioninternational.org/media/articles/witnessing-in-a-tb-sanitarium.

Questions for individual reflection or group discussion:

1. Reread Colossians 3:2–3. What do you think it means to set our hearts and minds on things above?

2. Jesus came to save *His people* from their sins. We often think only in terms of nonbelievers needing salvation. But Jesus knew that we needed salvation too! In Acts 2:47 we find these words: "And the Lord was adding to their number day by day those *who were being saved*." What areas of your life are still "being saved"?

3. God seldom gives us answers. Instead, He gives us promises. What does this mean and how have you found this to be true in your life?

4. Here is one of the greatest prayers we could ever pray: *May my thoughts please you today.* Discuss the words and close with the prayer.

CHAPTER 5

TALES OF HIDDEN SERVICE

Be careful not to practice your righteousness in front of others to be seen by them. If you do, you will have no reward from your Father in heaven.

Matthew 6:1 NIV

I love the legacy of the late Mother Teresa. Her reputation as a Nobel Peace Prize recipient and the founder of homes for the dying is well known. But it is her quiet acts of humility and tales of hidden service that have influenced me the most.

She once said, "What we do is but a drop in the ocean, but without that drop, the ocean would be less. We cannot do big things for God. We can only do small things with great love. That is what makes what we do something beautiful for God."

How often she would remind the nuns of her order to use their hearts and not just their hands. "Don't pass out meals with your hands. Pass them out with your heart. Don't wipe a table with a cloth. Use your heart."

So what might that look like for us?

- It might mean making the bed in the morning or washing the dishes after dinner for your wife.
- For you, perhaps it's finding the lowest employee on the totem pole at work and taking him to lunch.
- Or maybe it's setting up chairs without much ado.
- Or sweeping a hallway.
- Writing a note to someone, genuinely sharing how much he or she is appreciated without needing reciprocation.
- Giving someone credit rather than demanding it.
- Giving someone value who doesn't feel like they have much value.

And remember: True service is best if hidden.

Want to get back to the purity and simplicity of Jesus? Acts of hidden service help show us the way.

Right and Left Hands

Jesus was always careful not to do acts of service for the public to see, and He instructed His followers to do the same. Oh, don't get me wrong. Sometimes He did acts of service in public, but the acts of service were never done for the purpose of *being seen* while doing them. Jesus could have held a foot-washing ceremony during the feeding of the five thousand, for instance, in order to take advantage of a multitude seeing how humble He was. Instead He chose to wash the disciples' feet immediately following a private, closed meal for His twelve closest friends.

His example of privacy was His example of purity, and it is ours to follow.

Giving

The sixth chapter of Matthew, part of the Sermon on the Mount, points to this principle extensively. Jesus began this time of teaching by instructing His followers not to announce when they gave money to the needy. By contrast, the Pharisees were in the habit of announcing their giving in flashy, overt ways, even with fanfare and trumpet blowing. But Jesus said that the Pharisees had already received their reward in full.

> We can all begin service in secret by giving.

In fact, hidden service was so prized by Jesus that He explained it by using the literary technique of hyperbole, a purposeful exaggeration used to make a point:

> When you give to the needy, do not let your left hand know what your right hand is doing, so that your giving may be in secret. Then your Father, who sees what is done in secret, will reward you.
>
> Matthew 6:3–4 NIV

We can all begin service in secret by giving. Here are a few ways:

- Start tithing to your home church without reservation.
- Give a gift without regard to whether or not it is tax-deductible. Let Jesus dictate what and to whom you will give and not the IRS.
- Buy a journal for those who cannot afford one in order to encourage them in their pursuit of God.
- Give over and above your tithe toward a godly project without need for recognition.

Can you actually give with one hand without your other hand being aware of it? Of course not, yet the point is pressed for a reason. When it comes to acts of service, Jesus wants us always to err on the side of discretion rather than publication.

A few years back I wrote a book called *Leading on Empty*. It sold well, and a few months later a large royalty check arrived. I was thrilled. But on the way to the bank, the Lord spoke to my heart and said, "I want you to give the money to the ministry—the whole check."

My flesh rebelled and I squirmed. I tried to rationalize: "My family needs food. My car needs new tires! My roof needs repairing!" But all the spiritualizing couldn't make His voice go away. Oh, mind you, He doesn't yell. He doesn't nag. He just keeps His finger firmly on you. As the old saying goes, "You can run but you cannot hide." Not when it comes to God, anyway. You can twist and turn, but you can't shake the finger of God.

When I finally quit kicking, God said, "If you only wrote this book to make money, then your act of service wasn't for me. I want you to write for eternal reasons—to help lead others closer to me. Period."

He was right. Ever notice that? God is always right.

He wanted me to make sure that what I did was solely because God asked me to, not because I wanted something from it.

The twist to this story was that in the process I relearned yet another lesson: You can't out-give God. Friends, if you get into a giving contest with God, He will always win. Shortly after I signed away that check, my wife and I sold our house. The market at that time was on the upswing, and we ended up selling it for almost twice as much as we thought it would bring. The reward was more than I'd given away.

Praying

Similarly, Jesus instructed His followers in the act of praying privately. Some people loved to stand on street corners and pray in loud voices, hoping to be seen by others and praised for their acts of piety. But Jesus scorned such practices.

But when you pray, go into your room, close the door and pray to your Father, who is unseen. Then your Father, who sees what is done in secret, will reward you.

Matthew 6:6 NIV

In other words, it's better not to broadcast your level of devotion for Christ to others.

When I first came to Christ at nineteen, I attended a church that prayed. No, I mean PRAYED! We'd gather in a large room and people would pray at the top of their voices. When I entered the hallway leading up to the prayer room, it was already loud. But when I opened the door to enter, it was deafening! It was a yell fest for God. It was as if a contest to get God's attention was in session. The winner would be the one who prayed the loudest, longest, and fastest—without breathing.

I had to breathe, so I was somewhere near the back of the pack.

But later I realized that I needed to hear from God much more than He needed to hear from me! So often I made my prayers "listening times," where I would actually take out a notebook and listen to what the Holy Spirit was saying to me. I would ask Him questions and write down what I believed He was saying to me about each area:

- In what areas do I need help from others?
- How's my attitude been lately, Lord?
- In what areas do I need to improve?
- How am I doing in my marriage?
- How are my devotional times? Are they rich or are they becoming rote?
- Are there areas in my life or thinking that need renewal?

Of course there are times of public prayer where we will lead others, but there must be the balance of times of intimate prayer where we do heart checks and inside repair.

67

Fasting

Jesus used the same principle regarding fasting. In Jesus' day, some people purposely disfigured their faces when they fasted. They wanted to display the intensity of their devotion to God, to show the level of physical pain their devotion caused them. But Jesus told His followers to do the opposite.

> When you fast, put oil on your head and wash your face, so that it will not be obvious to others that you are fasting, but only to your Father, who is unseen; and your Father, who sees what is done in secret, will reward you.
>
> Matthew 6:17–18 NIV

Do you want to get closer to Jesus? Then follow in the footsteps of hidden service.

Cameras in the Soup Kitchen

The necessity of hidden service is especially true for those in positions of leadership. So often service is done only for ceremony. But that's not the way of the cross. How often have you seen a prominent leader putting on an apron in a soup kitchen only because the cameras are there? It's a photo op. As soon as the pictures are taken, off comes the apron.

Servanthood needs to be real.

As a leader, particularly an up-front leader, it's so easy to get a sense of entitlement, a false sense of importance, an attitude that "I'm the big cheese around here." But Jesus asks that we purposely *demote ourselves back to authenticity.* Mother Teresa once said, "Do you want to be great? Pick up a broom and sweep a floor."

That's the way home for servants.

That counterintuitiveness is why Jesus' message is so radical. Learn what it means to serve. Luke 22 reminds us that in the world, servanthood is what you start off with, and move away from as quickly as you can. But Jesus reminds us by His example that servanthood in the kingdom is something you have to *graduate to*.

> And there arose also a dispute among them as to which one of them was the greatest. And He said to them, ". . . The one who is greatest among you must become like the youngest, and the leader like the servant."
>
> Luke 22:24–26

In the kingdom, you have to be great in order to be a servant. Many may not qualify. It is the highest calling of all. You see, in order to be a servant, you must be great

- in patience
- in maturity
- in commitment
- in endurance
- in discipline
- in faith

In the kingdom, you have to be great in order to be a servant.

Not many can be servants, especially when we are tested. The greatest test of a servant is always how he responds when he is treated like one.

Many can serve—for a season—until it becomes work or until it becomes unrecognized or no longer appreciated by others. Of course, we must always remember to recognize and appreciate servants, but that is not what fuels true servants. It is simply the pure joy of being like Jesus and staying close to Him.

Jesus said in essence, "Who's the greater, the ones seated at the head table or the busboy serving?" Of course, we'd say, "It's the VIPs seated at the head table!"

Jesus counters, "But I am among you as the one who serves." (See Luke 22:27.)

If people are to see Jesus in our churches, we need to increase the servants, not the crowds. Often Jesus is obscured in the crowds. He is seen among servants.

Hugging the Lepers

Recently I participated in a documentary called *God in Hawaii*, where we traced the history of God's involvement in the islands. One of the sites we visited for the project was the leper colony on the island of Molokai. In 1873, Father Damien volunteered to be the first bishop of the colony and help care for the patients on the isolated island, many of whom were deformed, in despair, and without hope. Under his leadership, the colony of Kalaupapa was organized, and it began to flourish and prosper. Eventually, however, Father Damien contracted leprosy himself. He died in 1889 at the age of forty-nine.

Over the years, the colony has had some 8,000 patients. Today, there are just nine, all between the ages of eighty and ninety. They have all taken medication to arrest the disease, but it's impossible to reverse damage that's already been done, and many are scarred and disfigured.

I visited with one of the patients. He was a kind man in his upper eighties. He led the humble Bible study at the colony. Only a few attended, but he'd been leading it for many years. I saw his faithfulness to this tiny community on a lonely island in the middle of the Pacific.

I remembered a question God asked me once: "If I asked you to, could you serve me in obscurity for the rest of your life?"

I couldn't answer that. I mean, how could I disappear into a no-name country and pastor a small, no-name church until I died without anyone knowing who I was? It haunted me for a week or more before I finally surrendered to his theoretical request. But my need to be noticed was revealed, and I needed Him to wash me.

I quickly noticed that the leper patient's lower face was deformed and his hands were disfigured; several fingers were missing. But soon the harsh sentence of Hansen's disease faded as he recounted the years of his faithful ministry. He had been chosen to serve God in obscurity, and to him it was an honor.

At the close of our visit, I asked him if I could give him a hug. I figured there weren't too many people lining up to hug lepers.

He smiled and wrapped his arms around me. As we hugged I told him I would like to return and speak at his Bible study. He laughed and said, "We'll be waiting. All three of us!"

> He had been chosen to serve God in obscurity, and to him it was an honor.

I remember thinking that this is exactly the kind of thing we all need to do every day of our lives: Remember the forgotten people. I see people who serve at New Hope (the church I pastor) that I need to hug and remember. Maureen is one of them. She and her brother Kean are such precious people. I have known them for many years. Maureen has Down's syndrome, and I look forward to giving her a big hug each week. She can't speak much, but she sure can smile!

Following Christ is not about courting those who are able to give a big donation or who might be able to promote our cause or advance our social standing. The way of the cross is caring for those who would otherwise be forgotten.

The key to greatness is not found in campaigning for people's approval. It's making sure that in your life there are many tales of hidden service, where you demote yourself back to authenticity. Make sure you're walking where Jesus is walking.

You'll find Him when you serve.

God's Hidden Service

God is the One who began the program of hidden service. We find Him blessing, healing, and delivering without much fanfare. I wonder how many acts of service have been performed in secret for *my* sake? I wonder how many times my life was spared? I won't know until I'm in my celestial home. I wonder how many times

- I was spared from an accident by God's grace
- my marriage could have been destroyed if it weren't for His keeping power
- I was kept from an illness by God's healing power
- I was shielded from knowing about upcoming blessings in order to keep me dependent on Him lest I become proud.

Let's look at two lives that God served in secret ways by His grace.

Abraham

God knows that we are frail, that we are but dust, and He knows what we can handle and what would cause us to fail. He served Abraham in secret in order that he would remain dependent and humble. In His eternal wisdom, He conceals His workings only to reveal them one by one. In this way, we are given ample time to grow to the maturity necessary to sustain what God has in store for us.

> The Lord said, "Shall I hide from Abraham what I am about to do, since Abraham will surely become a great and mighty nation and in him all the nations of the earth will be blessed?"
>
> Genesis 18:17–18

As time went by and Abraham's faith grew, God would eventually reveal His plans to him. But in His wisdom, God waits until we not only are at a place to receive His blessing, but have sufficient character to steward what He entrusts to us.

Abimelech

Abimelech was the king of Gerar when Abraham and Sarah arrived. Sarah must have been quite attractive, because the king wanted to get to know this young woman. Although Abimelech was a warring king, it was universally accepted that no one took another man's wife. Adultery was out of the question. But because Abimelech was king . . . *murder* was not. If it became known that Sarah was married, Abimelech would simply kill Abraham, and Sarah would no longer be married!

So when Abraham was questioned about her relationship to him, he said, "She is my sister."

Abimelech took her into his home but did not have relations with her. In the course of the evening, God came to him in a dream and said in no uncertain terms: "Abimelech, you are a dead man because you have someone else's wife. And if you don't return her tomorrow, you and your household are finished!"

> I wonder how many acts of service have been performed in secret for my sake?

The following morning, Abimelech's first order of business was to return this woman to her husband. Abraham prayed for Abimelech, and we find these haunting words:

> God healed Abimelech and his wife and his maids, so that they bore children. For the Lord had closed fast all the wombs of the household of Abimelech because of Sarah.
>
> Genesis 20:17–18

Remember, this happened over the course of just two days, so the wombs of the women had been closed, but the women had not known it. But if God had not healed them, it would have been the end of the household of Abimelech. No more heirs. No more sounds of babies. No children playing in the streets. A generation would have aged and ended a lineage. But because Sarah was returned to Abraham, God healed the wombs and they were able to bear children again.

I wonder how many times God has healed us and we never even knew we were sick or were about to suffer a major setback. Perhaps even our death was preempted by His service in secret.

God does this all the time, and so must we. It's important for us to get back to God's example. When you pursue Him, He will be found among those who serve.

He is found in the servants' quarters—not on the stage.

Questions for individual reflection or group discussion:

1. The Bible describes how people sometimes do acts of righteousness only to be seen by others. Without naming names or organizations, have you seen examples of this today?

2. Reread Matthew 6:1. Why is it important that acts of service always bring attention to Christ and not to us?

3. Christians need to "demote themselves back to authenticity." What does this mean, and why is this action so vital?

4. How can you find Jesus when you serve?

5. Describe some hidden acts of service that you can do this week for those around you.

CHAPTER 6

ONE THING

You are worried and bothered about so many things; but only
one thing is necessary.

Luke 10:41–42

We live in a society where multitasking is the new normal. Cell
phones and laptop computers demand Wi-Fi accessibility everywhere. Mothers successfully parent three children and hold down
a full-time job while simultaneously managing the schedule of a
busy chauffeur. Yet in the heart of men and women is a yearning
for the simple, a hunger for an uncomplicated day, a craving for
purpose and focus and time to enjoy life.

But in the meantime, if you're a person who drives with one
knee on the steering wheel while talking on your cell phone
and drinking coffee, you'll need to know that you're in good
company.

Whose company?

Martha's.

No, not Martha Stewart. This Martha was probably older
than her two siblings, Mary and Lazarus. The rabbi who in

John 11 caused quite a stir among the religious elite by bringing Lazarus back from the dead was stopping by for a visit. The Scriptures aren't clear as to the chronology of these events, but in either case, there was a close bond between Jesus and this tight-knit family. We find in John 11:5 that "Jesus loved Martha and her sister and Lazarus." In Luke's account, we slip into an intimate scene where Jesus admonishes the multitasking sister of Mary. His instruction is not only for the type-A Marthas of the world, but for any of us who may need a little more focus and setting of priorities.

Martha was scurrying about the kitchen, while Mary had seated herself at the feet of Jesus listening to His words. When Martha complained about the obvious discrepancy between her diligence and Mary's leisure, we find these telling words:

> The Lord answered and said to her, "Martha, Martha, you are worried and bothered about so many things; but *only one thing is necessary,* for Mary has chosen the good part, which shall not be taken away from her."
>
> Luke 10:41–42 (emphasis added)

Did you catch that salient phrase?

"Only one thing is necessary."

We can easily become consumed by the demands that push us into the urgent until we find ourselves too fatigued to water our souls. The desert times are inevitable, but stopping frequently to drink deeply from the well found at His feet can be our only hope to outlast the demanding times ahead.

The story is told of a drought that inflicted a region of orange groves. Among the many orchards stood one grove whose trees remained green while the surrounding ones wilted and browned. When he was asked his secret, the grower gave this answer:

"My trees can go two more weeks without water. You see, when they were young, I would often withhold water from them so they had to send their roots down more deeply in order to drink. Now while others are browning, my trees are taking water from a source that is far deeper."

Mary had chosen the good part, and it was sitting at the feet of Jesus listening to His words. She had found the *one necessary treasure,* and when we do that, we begin the journey of a lifetime.

His Presence

Picture a dusty Middle-Eastern road winding through grape arbors, grasslands, and low-lying hills. It's a road of solitude. Among the few out traveling on this day are two men, disciples of Jesus. One is named Cleopas and the other man's name is lost in history. The two are journeying from the grand city of Jerusalem to a smaller village called Emmaus, seven miles away. Such a walk would last slightly more than two hours, about the length of a good movie today. Let's slip quietly into the scene found in the twenty-fourth chapter of Luke.

The men are caught in intense conversation, rehashing everything that's recently happened in Jerusalem. Their leader, Jesus of Nazareth, a prophet powerful in word and deed, was handed over to the rulers and sentenced to death. He was crucified between two thieves. Both disciples saw the whippings and beatings, the blood, the agony, and the shame of their leader's death. The news is the buzz of the town. The two men are overwhelmed by the events—distraught, discouraged, depressed.

Another man appears on the dirt road. Soon he approaches, kicking up a slight cloud of dust, joining them on their walk. The two don't recognize the man. He's young, bearded, an Israelite just like them. Wanting to join in their conversation, he queries, "May I ask what you have been discussing?"

Unable to navigate the simplicity of the question, they blurt: "Are you the only one in Jerusalem who doesn't know what has just taken place? You must be a visitor to the city!"

They still don't recognize who He is.

"Hmm . . . what events are those?" Jesus says.

(Pause a moment. Notice the humor and dry-witted understatement in Jesus' words.)

The men summarize their narrative to someone they deem out-of-touch with the breaking news. The unassuming Jesus replies:

> "Did not the Messiah have to suffer these things and then enter his glory?" And beginning with Moses and all the Prophets, he explained to them what was said in all the Scriptures concerning himself.
>
> Luke 24:26–27 NIV

It's a straightforward point Jesus is making, but it is a point easier stated than practiced. Simply put, if you understand the Scriptures, you understand the ways of God. The Scriptures are the way to get to know the very One who is walking with you. But if you don't understand the Scriptures, Jesus can be walking with you and you won't even recognize Him.

> **If you understand the Scriptures, you understand the ways of God.**

They walk farther and arrive at Emmaus, and Jesus acts like He's going to keep on walking, but the disciples ask Him to stay and have supper with them. It's during dinner that the two disciples' eyes are finally opened. Can you imagine their surprise? The shock? Their joy! *"Jesus! It's you! You're alive!"*

Instantly Jesus disappears from sight. But the news is out! That very hour the two disciples skedaddle back to Jerusalem, eager to tell what they've just seen. It's nighttime by now. The road is rocky. The two stumble along, sprinting in the dark. But they're so excited, they just can't wait. They rush back to tell everybody the good news that Jesus is alive

Contrast the marked difference in the disciples' outlook to and from Jerusalem.

On the way to Emmaus, Jesus was with them. They didn't recognize Him, but He was with them nonetheless. They were down-in-the-mouth, discouraged, and ready to give up. Then on the way back to Jerusalem, the two were excited, thrilled, animated, and anticipating talking to people about the risen Lord.

Now, Jesus was with them on the road back, as well, only this time by His Spirit. He was there with them *both ways*—on the way there, physically, and on the way back, spiritually. But what changed the disciples' outlook? It wasn't the presence of the Holy One; He was with them both ways. However, going to Emmaus they were discouraged. Returning, they were excited and full of joy. The change wasn't the presence of Christ.

It was the fact that they *recognized* the presence of Christ.

When we don't recognize the presence of Christ, life can be disheartening, but when we recognize that He is with us, it changes everything!

Getting back to Jesus is recognizing that you are, right now, in the presence of Christ. Acknowledge Him now. Greet Him. Whisper a welcome to Him just loud enough that you can hear yourself. Go ahead. Whisper, "I welcome you, Lord. I welcome you here into my life and I welcome you into my day."

It's time to get back to Jesus. How do we do that? Welcome Him.

He's wondering when you will recognize Him.

The Presence of Christ, the Word of God

One of the young people at our church asked me, "Pastor Wayne, have you ever heard the voice of God?"

"Yes," I said. "I hear Him all the time."

"No kidding? All the time?"

"Sure," I said. "What do you think the voice of God sounds like—an old man, a young man; what do you think?"

"I guess I don't know."

"God sounds just like the Bible."

The rest of the young people laughed but understood immediately what I was saying. The Bible is the very Word of God. It's the main vehicle God uses to communicate with us today.

If you will listen, you'll hear Him on every page of the Bible.

People often want God to speak audibly today, in a voice like Charlton Heston, I suppose—deep and bold and unmistakably divine. But I always tell people, if you can't recognize God speaking to you in the Bible, then there's no use in His talking to you audibly. Think about it—He's God! His audible voice would scare you half to death!

The invitation to us is to consistently discover the voice of God through the Bible. It needs to become an everyday regimen, something as familiar as breathing, chewing, or blinking. You might initially balk at this teaching. You've heard it before. It's nothing new. But I invite you to consider it anew.

Think about a professional musician. What must a pianist do to truly play her instrument? A fabulously gifted pianist doesn't do a lot of things. She just does a few of the same things over and over again. The secret to success is a daily regimen of repeated disciplines.

Pianists, especially, play scales repeatedly. Scales give a musician the ability to learn at a rapid rate, to progress, to recognize patterns, and to undertake great musical feats. Can you picture those scales? Pianists play the *do re mi fa so la ti do's*—ascending and descending notes, a progression of graduated steps going higher and lower in tone. They play major scales. They play minor scales. They play jazz scales and blues scales, classical scales, and non-Western scales. That's what they practice, again and again and again. They know that much of the tensile strength, speed, and eye/hand coordination they need is built not by playing Bach and Mozart, but by an everyday routine.

As a professional musician, if you've got your scales down, when somebody puts a Chopin in front of you with 32nd arpeggio notes, you can navigate those movements. But without the discipline that scales bring, that same composition will cause you to blink a couple of times and say, "Yikes! There are a lot of black dots on this page!"

Ignacy Jan Paderewski was a famous polish pianist. During World War I he was asked to be part of the war effort by playing concerts to raise money. He agreed, but he said to the state minister, "There's only one request. I will help with the war effort, but you must allow me to continue playing my scales three hours each day."

They agreed to the request but asked him why this was so important.

Here was his answer:

- If I miss one day of scales, when I play in a concert, I notice it.
- If I miss two days, the critics notice it.
- If I miss three days, the world notices it!

Like Children of the King

Now it shall come about that when [the king] sits on the throne of his kingdom, he shall write for himself a copy of this law on a scroll. . . . It shall be with him and he shall read it all the days of his life.

Deuteronomy 17:18–19

Moses reminds us how critical it was for the king to lead the people under the edict of God's voice, and His voice would be heard most clearly through the Law. And if it is good for the king, it's good for the king's kids!

I am often asked why the Bible is so stringent with the do's and don'ts, especially in the Old Testament.

Let me explain it as simply as I can.

The main problem with the Israelites was not their brains. It was their hearts. And they were quite adept at hiding the unclean motives of their hearts under religious trappings. God's target was their hearts, not their knowledge. They had the right answers and knew how to play the system, but God knew that unless their hearts were changed, they would stray as soon as they were given the chance.

Galatians 3:22–23 tells us:

> But the Scripture has shut up everyone under sin, so that the promise by faith in Jesus Christ might be given to those who believe. But before faith came, we were kept in custody under the law. . . . Therefore the Law has become our tutor to lead us to Christ.

The only way the true hearts of the Israelites could be revealed was through God putting the pressure on them. Acres and acres of freedom would allow their hearts of disobedience and rebellion to breed and spread. But when God narrowed the borders, they started kicking and squirming! It was only under the restrictive conditions of the Law that their selfish hearts would surface. Under constricting laws, the Israelites would be faced with their own disobedience.

But His laws were not an expression of His narrowness. They manifested the loving heart of a father.

When my son Aaron was five and his sister Amy was six, sibling rivalry was in full bloom. It started with an argue-fest and escalated into a full-scale battle. One day they had graduated to throwing blows when the commotion caught my attention.

By the time I arrived at the scene of the crime, Aaron was ready for a fight to the death.

"I hate her. I hate this family. I hate everybody!"

I knew he was about to do something that he might later regret, so I grabbed him and held him tightly against me to keep him from attacking his sister (who was ready to mark him for life with her fingernails).

I imprisoned his little body in a full embrace as he continued his diatribe. "I can't stand her. Let me go and I will let her know who's boss! I hate her!"

I held him snugly and replied, "But we love you. So settle down. I'm not letting go until you settle down!"

Every so often, one of his arms would escape or a leg would kick and I'd tuck it back into the cocoon of control.

"You're OK," I'd assure him. "Settle down and Dad will let you go, but not before." He'd kick out and his little arms would flail, but I held on to him securely until I felt his body relax. Within moments, I heard his sobs and the tears began to flow.

"Dad loves you, son. And this is your family. We all have differences, but that doesn't mean we will hurt one another. Is that what you want to do?"

"No, Dad," he sobbed. "I'm sorry."

"OK, Dad will let you go but you need to relax. You got it?"

"Yes. I'm sorry."

At that moment I knew I could increase his freedom because his heart was different. But until his heart changed, I had to restrict his actions, not by anger but by my love.

> Do not be afraid, little flock, for your Father has chosen gladly
> to give you the kingdom.
>
> Luke 12:32

God's desire is to give His children full freedom and complete liberty, but that is only available when He has garnered not only our minds, but our hearts.

His transforming embrace is the same as His *reforming* embrace.

In the beginning, God's Word was indeed stringent, but it was His way of holding us tightly to Him until our rebellion was revealed and reformed. His laws were designed to expose and expunge selfish hearts, and when the tutoring was complete, the promises of Christ would be delivered to those whose hearts had been transformed by His embrace.

Unforced Rhythms

A few years back, when I was burning out in pastoral ministry, I went away for a few days to a "no talking" monastery. When I was finished there, I came to Oregon to spend another twenty-some days alone with God—sitting, reading, thinking, and praying—trying to regain my physical and spiritual equilibrium.

At first glance, that extended time away was not simple for me. I needed to drastically rearrange my schedule. During those weeks away I needed to consciously decide not to return phone calls, prepare messages, counsel people, plan projects, or do research for upcoming talks, books, or church events. I noticed that Jesus took regular and extended times away to be with the Father.

> In solitude, I relearned to recognize the presence of God.

Oddly enough, what Jesus found so normal in His course of ministry, I found very abnormal.

Those weeks alone with God proved life-changing for me. In solitude, I relearned to recognize the presence of God. God was not commanding me onward. He wasn't pushing me toward the brink of exhaustion. That was all my doing. God was inviting me to a new way of living, one that was freer, unforced.

Jesus offers to you this same invitation:

> Are you tired? Worn out? Burned out on religion? Come to me. Get away with me and you'll recover your life. I'll show you how to take a real rest. Walk with me and work with me—watch how I do it. Learn the unforced rhythms of grace. I won't lay anything heavy or ill-fitting on you. Keep company with me and you'll learn to live freely and lightly.
>
> Matthew 11:28–30 THE MESSAGE

How do we follow Christ in this manner, learning to live freely and lightly in the unforced rhythms of grace?

Let me suggest four important principles for growing closer to God through Scripture.

1. Read the Bible Daily

Go directly to Scripture. Sure, we all love *Our Daily Bread, My Utmost for His Highest,* and other devotional books. But as wonderful as devotional aids can be, the Bible is the only book that's inspired by God (2 Timothy 3:16).

Read the Bible daily with the little word SOAP in mind. That's an acronym for:

- Scripture
- Observation
- Application
- Prayer

The method is simple. Pick a portion of Scripture and read it. Read it twice or even three times if needed. Focus on the message.

Next, do some careful observing and consideration. Ponder

the message God has highlighted for you. You may want to write out what you observe. Ask yourself what's happening, who's affected, and what's taking place.

Then take some time to consider how you plan to put into practice the message God has brought to your attention. How will you be different today as a result of what you've read? Application is a vital part of the process. Without it, you're simply amassing information.

The final stage of the process is prayer. Your conversation doesn't need to be long. Ask God to help you apply what you've just learned. And don't forget to soak your prayer in thanksgiving.

> In every situation, by prayer and petition, with thanksgiving, present your requests to God.
>
> Philippians 4:6 NIV

2. Regularly Take Time for Solitude

Solitude is different from *isolation*. Isolation is what a person typically seeks when he's so burned out he doesn't want to be around anybody. On a scale of minus ten to positive ten, he's at a minus twelve. And he just needs to get away from people.

After the stint in isolation is done, a person has come from a minus twelve to a zero. The problem then is that he often goes back out in public without ever advancing beyond zero. He hasn't gained wisdom.

Solitude is an intentional recharging process. When your tank is low, solitude helps you come back at a plus ten.

Most of us wait until we're completely depleted and spent before we get away. So we go into isolation. That can be helpful. But isolation is only therapy. Healing. Triage.

Solitude, however, is a chosen time to get alone. We find this in Luke 4, where Jesus was compelled by the Spirit to go into the wilderness for forty days. There, He was tempted by the devil. Jesus overcame every temptation. Note that Luke records how Jesus was led into the desert *full* of the Holy Spirit (Luke 4:1). But when the time was over, He returned to Galilee *in the power of the Spirit* (Luke 4:14). It's one thing to be compelled by the Spirit. It's another thing to be empowered by the Spirit. Empowerment requires a time of solitude. When Jesus came back from the wilderness in the power of the Spirit, that's when He began His ministry.

The length of your time of solitude depends on your schedule as well as what projects are coming up ahead of you. Your schedule may only allow a day or two of solitude. Then take it. But sometimes you'll have a very large, important event or season that you know you need to prepare for. That requires solitude beforehand.

For example, I was gone from our church in Hawaii for two and a half years while I was rebuilding our Bible college in Eugene, Oregon. When that season was complete, I found that I desperately needed to spend more time in solitude. I needed to get away alone to think, to pray, and to hear afresh from God.

I call them *Sabbath moments.*

Sabbath moments are when you take a day or two, or even an afternoon, and spend it in planned solitude. Sometimes I just take my Bible and go off on my motorcycle for a few hours. Other times I'll go for three days. I take a Bible, a journal, and my calendar. I go to think, pray, and plan. The first day I work out, walk, or run. I often fast by just drinking liquids. And then I do long devotions.

By the second morning, God begins revealing things to me. I read the Word and slowly let it speak to me. There's a big difference between studying the Word and letting the Word study you. The first morning I'm doing Bible study. By the second or third morning, the Bible is studying me. Nothing hidden. Nothing held back. Nothing rationalized. Nothing excused.

At that point, I start to ask myself the tough questions:

- How am I doing as a man of God when no one is looking?
- How am I doing in my marriage . . . really?
- How am I doing in my attitude?
- How am I doing as a dad?
- How am I doing in my thought life?

3. Immerse Yourself in Gratefulness

The last time I got away was for four days. The theme that God spoke to me about was gratefulness. I was still involved in ministry, but I realized I wasn't grateful anymore. That's when my joy quotient starts to go south and motives get skewed. When that happens, we are destined to slowly go blind.

> It is only as we renew our hearts of gratefulness that our eyesight is restored.

It is only as we renew our hearts of gratefulness that our eyesight is restored.

If you lose gratefulness, you can still have a good job, friends, a house, fine children, and a supportive wife. But if you are no longer expressing gratefulness, you'll go blind to God's workings and blessings.

When you're grateful, God will do everything He can to give you more. The psalmist knew this well. He proclaims, "Enter His gates with thanksgiving and His courts with praise" (Psalm 100:4).

Why? He continues: "For the Lord is good" (v. 5).

Lose your sense of gratefulness and eventually everything you have erodes.

I remember one afternoon when my son Aaron was seven

years old. He ambled up the driveway with a friend in tow. I was working on my car when I noticed the chain on his friend's bicycle dragging.

"Dad," Aaron said, "my friend's bike doesn't work anymore."

I saw the problem immediately—his friend's bicycle chain had fallen off the back sprocket—and I knew it was an easy fix. But my mischievous nature wanted to play with them a bit. "Fix it? Wow," I said thoughtfully. "Looks really bad. Usually when these things happen, we've just got to throw the bike away."

"But, Dad," Aaron said. "It's not that old of a bike. And he's my friend!"

"Well," I said, scratching my head. "It looks like the flux capacitor's shot and the spiral separator is dislocated from the reactive generator."

The blank stares of innocence told me that my drama was working.

"But because you two look like good kids, I'm going to do everything I can do to fix this."

I'll never forget it. Aaron turned to his friend and said, "Watch this! My dad can do anything!"

I was so tickled by his response and proud to be his dad. After that kind of a grateful response, I didn't only want to fix the chain. I fancied the thought of pinstriping his bike and decking it out with a new radio, basket, and headlights. And maybe even affixing some playing cards to the spokes until it sounded like a Harley Ultra Glide with open pipes!

Our heavenly Father is the same way when we express our grateful hearts for what He's done.

4. Regularly Take Time for Reflection

We don't learn from experiences. We learn from *reflecting* on those experiences.

The key is reconsidering the responses you had to an event. Reflection is not rehashing old mistakes. It's meditating on what God has taught you through those mistakes.

Some people's lives are like blank books, where they never write anything down or reflect upon it.

Other people's lives are like diaries. They write their experiences down—the good, the bad, and the ugly—but they never reflect upon them. They simply record them.

But the lives that are the richest are those whose lives are like daily journals. They record the events, and then they review what they've learned from those events. They invest the time to reflect on their experiences. That's one of the richest fields from which we can mine gems of wisdom.

People ask me if I have made major mistakes.

I've made millions of them, but the question is not whether I've made mistakes. The question is what have I done with those mistakes?

When I err (which seems to happen daily for me), I take time to reflect on it. I wring it and squeeze every bit of wisdom out of it that I can. I tuck those lessons away in my heart for future reference and growth.

This next step is awfully important. I then throw the empty shell of the experience over my shoulder and don't give it another thought.

Learn from your past. Make it your mentor. I choose to make my past a tutor, not a torturer. Your past can be a mile marker or a hitching post. If it becomes a hitching post, you are tied to your past. When you reflect on it, it becomes a mile marker that leaves you with a clearer sense of direction for your future.

Time to Drink Again From the Source

The book *A Distant Grief* by F. Kefa Sempangi describes his time as a pastor in Uganda in the 1970s under the dictator Idi

Amin. Slaughter and destruction characterized the country during that season. As a young minister, Sempangi witnessed the slayings. To escape the maltreatment, he fled with his family to America. There, he studied theology, earned a seminary degree, and continued to minister. Years later with the war a distant memory, his life became peaceful, still, safe, and sheltered.

It was on a sultry afternoon while sitting in his sheltered office that he realized that something in him had died.

In Uganda, hearing God for his daily ration of hope was not an option. But in this new country, the urgency he once knew didn't seem so important. In Uganda, he had no guarantee of tomorrow. But now, each morning started just like the one before. In his former country of persecution, Sempangi read the Word for his very existence. In America, he read the Bible to analyze texts and speculate about meaning. He had come to enjoy abstract theological discussions. He no longer read the Bible to see Jesus. Fellowship with other believers revolved around ideas rather than the vital work of Christ in their lives.

The stagnant water of religious activity or even ministry involvement alone becomes acrid and stale. It will never quench the thirsting of your soul. Press your roots deeper, and when times of drought come, and they will, you will find a refreshing that's only available from one Source.

It's time to get back to Jesus.

Open the Bible. It reveals the Source to satisfy your thirsty soul.

Questions for individual reflection or group discussion:

1. Have you ever heard the voice of God? What was it like? Has it changed the way you live?

2. What about those who have never heard the audible voice of God? What does that mean?

3. In John 20:29, we read: "Jesus said to him, 'Because you have seen Me, have you believed? Blessed are they who did not see, and yet believed.'" What does this mean for us today?

4. How is maintaining a regular devotional life like a professional musician constantly working on scales?

5. What does the acronym SOAP stand for, and why is this method of reading the Bible both simple and effective?

6. What are the blessings of a daily discipline in the Word and what are the dangers?

7. Come prepared to share one of your devotional entries.

8. Why is it important to regularly take time for reflection?

CHAPTER 7

EYES ON
THE HARVEST

The harvest is plentiful, but the workers are few. Therefore
beseech the Lord of the harvest to send out workers into His
harvest.

Matthew 9:37–38

I often tell my granddaughter, Elliana, how to pray. If I don't
guide her, she will pray for the world, the universe, the cats, and
the cars that go by the house. But if I can keep her on track, we
will be able to have dinner before the clock strikes twelve. I am
certain that she will be the head of our prayer ministry in years
to come. But I have about twenty years to plan and prepare.
Until then, I'll keep guiding her prayers before dinner.

Jesus guides our prayers too. The disciples once said, "Lord,
teach us to pray" (Luke 11:1). I wouldn't mind taking a prayer
seminar taught by the Master.

We still can.

Slip into one of the seminars the disciples were attending. You can hear Him instruct them on how to pray.

"Pray therefore to the Lord of the harvest, that he will send forth laborers into his harvest. The harvest is ready but the laborers are not" (see Matthew 9:37–38).

I wonder how many prayers of mine Jesus has answered.

A hundred?

A thousand?

Maybe it's time we answered just one of His.

Consider this chapter an invitation to regain focus. It's a call to get our eyes back on Jesus and the things He cared about, to get our eyes back on the harvest. I'll bet most of us pray often for our own needs, but consider this a divine request to pray for others' greatest need: salvation.

Pretty simple.

Let Him guide your prayers. Otherwise you may be praying for dogs, cats, and cars.

Jesus always had His eyes on the harvest. He didn't pray for more money, fewer problems, or bigger houses very often. Reading the Bible, I notice that He didn't pray for more friends, more prominence, or more blessings. He never told the disciples to pray for a problem-free life, a fat retirement account, or a pin-striped donkey that would get them down the road faster and in style.

> **Jesus didn't pray for more money, fewer problems, or bigger houses.**

In Luke 10, Jesus told His disciples to pray fervently for laborers who had their eyes on the harvest.

That same simple directive is ours.

It's easy to lose focus in a mega-church, or in any church for that matter. Weekend services just seem to happen on cue, and programs appear to take place automatically without much prompting. The lights come on, people sing songs and play instruments that just happen to be in tune, and they seem to play in rhythm . . . usually. The preacher comes up with an encouraging sermon and the right Scriptures just materialize on the screens. We pray for God's blessings and after a rousing final chorus, we leave for lunch, inspired to face another week at work.

We punched our spiritual time cards, and we motor onward in our daily lives.

But we forgot our assignment.

The weekend service was not an end. It was a means to partner with one another in our attempts to reach our families and friends for Christ. It's not just about Jesus working in us. It's also about Jesus working *through* us.

You never determine the size of a church by how many are in it. You measure its size by how many are still outside of its doors.

Stay Near the Door

In the early part of the twentieth century, the Reverend Samuel Shoemaker was known as one of the ten greatest preachers in America. He was rector of the Calvary Protestant Episcopal Church in New York in the 1920s and later the rector of the Calvary Episcopal Church in Pittsburgh. He was also one of the spiritual leaders who helped draft the original Twelve Steps of Alcoholics Anonymous, and was a spiritual teacher to Bill Wilson, AA's co-founder.

Those who knew Shoemaker best described how his entire life was dedicated to showing people how to find God. He penned several versions of a poem titled "So I Stay Near the Door," which begins:

> I stay near the door.
> I neither go too far in, nor stay too far out.[1]

1. Reverend Samuel Shoemaker, "So I Stay Near the Door," in Helen Shoemaker, *I Stand by the Door* (Waco, TX: Word, 1967).

He was speaking of the door to a relationship with God, and his aim was to be where he could show others the way. That's the key for us as well—to stay near to where people are receiving Christ.

Stay near the door.

There's Always One in the Crowd

It was a busy day and the arrival of the miracle worker had people lining the street as if it were a Fourth of July parade. Mark 5 records the event with a focus on one woman caught in the press of the crowd. In the middle of the jumble, Jesus stopped and asked, "Who touched Me?"

The disciples were confused. "Who touched you?" they answered. "We are being pressed on all sides by humanity! It's a madhouse! Everybody's bumping into You!"

"No," Jesus replied. "Somebody *touched* Me."

I can see the disciples shaking their heads. They were stifled by the crowds and stumped by His question.

"I felt power go out of Me."

Just then, a woman fell down before Him and admitted that she had reached out and touched the hem of His garment. Quickly she explained that for many years she had suffered from an affliction. Worn and depleted, she had pinned all her hopes on the mercy of the miracle worker. Jesus stopped the parade and said, "Go your way. Your faith has made you well" (see Mark 5:25–32).

There's a difference between bumping into Jesus and *touching* Him. And for Jesus, that will stop the parade. He took the time to recognize that touch among the hundreds of bumps, and paused to bring healing to this woman who came knocking.

There will be many who are bumping into Jesus each weekend, but there may be only one or two that are reaching for help.

Stay near the door.

Baptisms and an Orange Robe

Our church has grown quite a bit since its inception, and there are quite a few notables who attend: prominent officials in government, influencers in business, and many who are skilled in the arts. I'm thrilled that our church reaches all types of people, including well-known ones, but we would be far wide of the mark to think that our church only exists to reach the "important" ones.

A few weeks ago we held a baptism. I like to joke that we baptize in the largest baptismal pool in the U.S., the Pacific Ocean. That particular Sunday afternoon, we were baptizing just over a hundred people. The service is held in an open-air public venue, so it was hard to tell a regular from a visitor, and a veteran from one who was simply strolling by.

A few minutes before the service began, I noticed a middle-aged man mingling among the crowd. I had never seen him before, and I had no idea if he was connected to our church, if he had lost his way, or if he had just stopped by for a meal. He was as round as he was tall with a friendly face that reminded me of the kind-faced monk in *Robin Hood* known as Little John.

Most strikingly, he was clothed in a bright orange robe.

Under his arm was tucked a large conch shell. "Would you like to hear it?" he said excitedly. "Go for it!" I said, and that he did!

Now if you know how to blow one of these abandoned crustacean dwellings, its romantic sounds can remind you of a moonlit evening on a South Pacific island.

Blown poorly, however, it will resemble the bellowing of a pregnant cow.

You see the risk?

"By the way," he asked before his audition, "would you mind if I blow my conch when people come out of the water after having been baptized?"

In more than thirty years of pastoral ministry, this was a first for me. I usually think pretty fast on my feet, but on this one, I was stumped. I figured the most pastoral thing I could do was . . . to pass the buck to another pastor. I told him that I would be happy to introduce him to our worship leader, who was standing about fifty feet away.

Our music director was leading a small band of worshipers on a nearby stretch of sand. Upon arriving, I told my newfound friend to repeat his request. After hearing "Little John's" appeal, I heard the music director reply, "Sure! We'll work that right into our arrangement!"

I smiled.

Deliverance!

I stepped into the ocean. We prayed with each one, and when the candidate arose from his or her watery grave, I could hear a sound coming over the waters. But it wasn't the sound of a bovine. It was like the blast of many trumpets. It had a ring of triumph, a sound of victory.

Later on I discovered something precious . . .

Right by the door.

One of the ministries we have at New Hope is led by a dear woman, Carolina. She leads a ministry to marginalized people: the homeless, hurting, forgotten, and disabled. It turned out that the man in the robe, Andrew, worked with Carolina's ministry. Andrew had brought six people with him to be baptized that day. Three were in wheelchairs, one was hunched over from scoliosis of the spine, and another was unable to speak.

And there was Frank.

I noticed that one of Frank's arms hung limp by his side, but it didn't seem to hamper him at all. I learned that Frank had lived for more than eleven years under a bridge near the highway. He had recently received Christ and was excited about his faith. Interestingly he wasn't only homeless, he was a leader among the homeless. (I wasn't aware that such a thing existed.) Frank explained that sometimes homeless camps can be quite organized.

"You know," said Andrew, "Frank could help us lead many homeless people to Christ."

We baptized Frank that day. I found him later among the crowd and gave him a hug. We talked for a long time afterward, and as the afternoon sun stretched its long, pastel arms over the waters, I noticed the calm radiance that came over Frank.

You can tell the difference between the surface smiles and the deep ones.

"Frank," I said, "do you think that one day we could take a music group under the bridge and hold an evangelistic festival for the bridge people?"

"That would be just wonderful," he said.

So that day another ministry began to emerge. Frank is now a wonderful volunteer leader at the church, and I look forward to his helping us reach homeless people for Christ.

Frank stays near the door.

It would have been so easy in the beginning for me to judge Andrew with his orange robe as an oddball, a throwaway person. But in actuality he was a minister of the gospel reaching the ones I had forgotten.

Andrew stayed near the door.

It's always a temptation for a church to keep its reputation shiny and polished, but that's not necessarily who we are. We welcome the VIPs, but we stay near the door for the one or two who are hidden by the crowd and silently reaching toward His hem. If our eyes are on the harvest, we won't miss a Frank, an Andrew, or anyone else He'd stop the parade for.

> If our eyes are on the harvest, we won't miss a Frank, an Andrew, or anyone else He'd stop the parade for.

Consider that throughout much of the Bible, Jesus reached out to bridge people—like a woman caught in adultery and a leper ringing a bell, crying, "Unclean!" He loved the lame man, the one with the withered hand, the blind, and the disabled by the pool of Bethesda.

The harvest comes in ways least expected.

That's why Jesus stayed near the door.

The Face in Front of You

You may be a businessperson, a college student, or a housewife, and you can't go into your work, school, or neighborhood and hold an evangelistic crusade. It just won't fly in your particular subculture.

So where do you start?

Start where Mother Teresa suggested. Begin with the face that's in front of you. It could be a neighbor, family member, a teacher at your child's school, the co-worker in the cubicle next to you, or the checkout clerk at the supermarket. When paths cross, never define it as *coincidence*.

There is no randomness with God.

When we're near the door, three main strategies will guide us in helping bring people a step closer to Jesus.

1. Understand the "Nudge"

Think of a "nudge" as a small prod you give another person toward Christ. It might just be a word of encouragement or a whispered reassurance. A nudge has no great goal or agenda in mind. It's not an altar call or thrashing an unsuspecting pagan with a family Bible.

It's a small encouragement. The reminder of a promise. The hint of your support.

You don't wait for a response. No reply necessary. You simply plant a seed and wander off.

There was a tiny Filipino woman in our condo who cleaned the carpets. She came as quietly as she left. I passed by her in the hallway of our building week after week but never asked her name or paid much attention. One day I thought, "Today I'm going to make an effort to ask her name when I see her."

I noticed her cleaning the hallway, so I made a detour to talk with her. That was all. Consider it a nudge. No great agenda. No ulterior motive. Simply nothing other than to let her know she was appreciated and her efforts at keeping the common areas clean did not go unnoticed.

Think of it this way: Around the neck of every person is a big sign that reads: "Please help me to feel valuable today."

So I did.

The following week she remembered me, and I remembered her name. I could now greet her by name, and this I did for several weeks.

Not long after that, I noticed her showing up in church. And a few months later at our Easter services, she received Christ.

It all started by stopping and noticing her because maybe she was secretly stretching toward the hem of His garment.

That's why I need to stand by the door.

People are passing by the door of the kingdom, but they don't realize they can enter in. They need someone to help them step through the passageway.

It didn't take a city crusade for that woman to find Jesus. It just took a nudge.

2. Tell the Story of Your Life

We proclaim to you what we have seen and heard, so that you also may have fellowship with us.

1 John 1:3 NIV

A person's testimony is one of the most powerful things he has. People can't deny or disbelieve your story, because your story is indisputably yours. A testimony involves three simple components: what your life was before you came to Christ, how you came to Christ, and how your life is different today.

There's an old hymn that reminds me of my testimony before Christ and after He came into my life. It proclaims, "This is my story. This is my song!"

I encourage everybody to be able tell their testimony in sixty seconds. Do you remember that thrilling movie with the fantastic race scenes called *Gone in 60 Seconds*? If you take longer than sixty seconds, the person you're talking to is gone. Be able to quickly articulate the spiritual story of your life.

I usually tell people about the time in my life when I began to get some spiritual curiosity. Often in people's lives that curiosity begins when there's a hurt or a sickness. My spiritual curiosity began when I was a sophomore in high school. My mother and father had divorced. I had moved to Oregon with my father, and my mother was in Hawaii. She was dying. I talked to my dad and asked him to send me to visit her before she died. Their relationship hadn't been riding on smooth seas toward the end, so he told me to wait until a later date when he could save some money.

Two days later I got a telegram saying my mother had passed away.

In anger against my father and anger against God, I walked the other way and got involved with drugs and an illicit lifestyle. I simply hated everything about God. He had taken my mother.

Time passed.

One day in college, someone invited me to a concert. I loved music. It was a Christian concert, but still I reluctantly went. I heard the musicians' testimonies, and their lives mirrored mine.

I realized that I was not alone in the struggles of life. That's when my heart began to soften toward Jesus. I was nineteen.

My life is completely different today.

When I share my testimony, that's about all I ever say. It's a very simple presentation. Some people say, "Oh, that's nice for you," and that's all there is to their response. But for other people, it's an eternal beginning. They simply need an example of a life transformed.

Maybe you think you don't have a testimony because you've always lived a moral lifestyle. In your mind a testimony is a highly dramatic story about how evil a person was before coming to Christ, and then how a person's life was miraculously changed. Perhaps you became a Christian when you were four.

Every believer has a testimony. The focus of a testimony is not what you were; it's who you are now in Christ. Why is Jesus important to you now? Talk about that.

It doesn't matter what end of the pit we're from. We're all from the pit. It doesn't matter.

Just stay near the door.

Sometimes we give the greatest applause and adulation in our churches to those who have come a long way out of the muck and mire, but we don't pay any attention to those who have one of the greatest awards heaven will ever present.

Every believer has a testimony.

My father, who had a lifetime career in the army, served under General MacArthur during World War II and was a prisoner during the Korean War. He prominently displayed the Silver Star he received for his acts of valor. Beside it hung a Bronze Star. He had a Purple Heart, and other ribbons for merit.

These are prestigious awards, but there's one award the Bible describes in Revelation that many of us may never receive. It's an esteemed award given only to those who steer clear of the enemy's abysmal compromises by which so many of us have been snagged.

Revelation 2:27–29 describes the reward as "the morning star." It's given to those who have overcome and who never involved themselves with the "deep things of Satan."

Think about it.

What a wonderful thing for a young person to say: "From an early age, I knew that Christ was the way. And if I had to choose Him all over again, I'd do it again in a heartbeat."

3. Offer the Invitation

An invitation involves deliberately asking a person to go somewhere spiritually. It may begin with a trip to church, a Christian concert, or even a Bible study. Ultimately, the invitation is a step closer to Christ. It's asking a person to make a move of faith.

It's a nudge and a follow-up.

This is a step that should never be forced upon a person. If they say no, they're not ready. But once the invitation is given, they begin to consider Christ more seriously. That's all God ever asks of you—to be faithful to do the inviting. And no matter how they respond, at least an invitation gets them thinking.

An invitation is similar to what God did with Jeremiah. In Jeremiah 18:2, God was talking with the prophet and invited him down to the potter's house, where more information would be given him. "There I will announce My words to you," said God.

Why would God invite Jeremiah to go somewhere else? God was already talking with Jeremiah in one location. Why would God want Jeremiah to go somewhere else?

At the potter's house, God was able to give Jeremiah a graphic presentation of His Word and His ways. Jeremiah saw firsthand the clay spinning on the wheel, the decisions the potter made concerning the clay, and how the clay belonged to the potter, not the other way around.

That was why Jeremiah needed to change locations. It brought spiritual truth into a new light.

Similarly, a person may be invited to a church service where a song or drama or message will touch that person's heart and confirm or ratify what's already been said. The person is able to see the ways of God in a new form.

Now, an invitation to another location isn't always needed. I've led some to Christ in restaurants and parking lots. If a person is ready, a person is ready. But often an invitation to another location, where a spiritually oriented event is taking place, will open the doorway even further.

There is no complicated strategy to inviting a person to an event. You just say, "Hey, we've got a concert coming up. Would you like to go?"

Similarly, there is no complicated strategy to inviting someone directly to Christ. People are often worried about what they might say. But I would encourage you that if you're speaking directly with a person about Jesus, and they're open to the conversation, there's probably not a wrong move you could make.

By way of example, when I give people an invitation to Christ, four components are usually involved. You don't have to use these. But I've often found them helpful.

- First, I say, **"Would you like to know more about Christ?"** Here I'm simply gaining permission to begin the process. If the person says no, then fine. But if a person says yes, I share my own testimony of how Jesus changed my life. I try to do this in sixty seconds. IF they are open and searching, I share a bit more about Jesus. Then I ask a second question . . .

- **"Would you like to open your heart and invite Him to begin a work inside of you?"** This is asking if the person is willing to give God a chance. Really, the burden here is put on God, not you as the presenter. You're letting the Holy Spirit reveal God to the person. The work is not even on the person as the responder. The question is simply, "Are you willing to let God do His work?" Often they say, "Yes, I'm willing to give Him a chance." So then I ask a third question . . .

- **"Can I pray for you?"** If yes, I pray a very simply prayer:

> *Lord Jesus, my friend here is opening*
> *his heart to you.*
> *I pray that you would reveal yourself to him this week.*
> *In Christ's name.*
> *Amen.*

Note that this is not a prayer for someone to fall on their knees and cry out to God. It's simply a prayer that invites Christ to begin His work.

Then I meet with the person the following week, which opens the door wider. Often the person's spiritual curiosity is piqued by then, so I ask a final question . . .

- **"Would you like the Lord to take over your life, and would you allow Him to change and transform you?"** Often they'll say yes at this point, because now they're open. So I pray the sinner's prayer with them and lead them to Christ. Something as simple as:

> *Lord Jesus, please come into my heart.*
> *Would you forgive me of my sins?*
> *My life is checkered with past mistakes*
> *where I've rejected you.*
> *But today I've changed my mind about that.*
> *Take over my life. Do what you need to in me.*
> *I choose to cooperate, and I call you Lord and Savior.*
> *Amen.*

Keep in mind that the ultimate success here is never up to us. God only asks that we are faithful. I've asked people if they want to give their lives to Christ and had them say no. The responsibility for a person's response does not lie with me. God simply invites me to be part of His kingdom work.

Eyes on the Harvest

In John 4:34–35 (NIV) Jesus said:

> My food is to do the will of him who sent me and to finish his work. Don't you have a saying, "It's still four months until harvest"? I tell you, open your eyes and look at the fields! They are ripe for harvest.

That phrase—*open your eyes*—is so important. Jesus wouldn't have said that unless there was a reason. If we have been inflicted by the disease of misguided devotion, our eyes will be closed to that which truly matters. Jesus invites us to open our eyes. The fields are ripe for harvest!

Have you ever thought about the true size of your church? A church isn't measured by how many people fill the pews each Sunday. It's measured by how many are still outside! You might be in a church of a thousand, but if you're in a city of one million, then the church is still fledgling.

Sometimes we get our eyes fixed on what we've already harvested. That's why Jesus said, "Lift up your eyes and look on the fields" (John 4:35). He reminds us to *lift up our eyes* because we more often than not have our eyes fixed on what we already have rather than on what is still standing in the fields.

The harvest will not self-reap, but it will self-destruct if not reaped.

How do you place your eyes back on the harvest? You can start by asking yourself questions such as:

- Does my neighbor know Christ?
- What family members of mine do not yet know Jesus?
- Are there colleagues at work who are far from God?
- Whose lives intersect with mine? Can I spend a few minutes a day to give them value?
- And in due time, can I help them find the door?

Look for opportunities to give people nudges toward Christ, to share your testimony, to give people invitations to spiritual events, and to invite people to follow Jesus.

The Power of an Invitation

An old Hebrew saying was highlighted in the poignant film *Schindler's List*. It says, "*Whoever saves one life saves the world entire.*"

If everyone reached a neighbor, we could win an entire community, and that is the gateway to the entire city. Never forget that just one invitation can open the door to the world.

Never underestimate the power of one invitation.

His name was Edward Kimball. He was a Sunday school teacher who talked with a young shoe-store clerk named Dwight. As a result Dwight received Christ. Dwight L. Moody grew into one of our country's greatest evangelists. Later, D. L. Moody talked to a man named J. Wilbur Chapman and encouraged him in his faith. J. Wilbur Chapman began holding evangelistic meetings, and a baseball-playing friend named Billy Sunday assisted him. Billy Sunday then held his own evangelistic meetings in Charlotte, North Carolina. The Charlotte Businessmen's Club grew out of those meetings. The club invited a man named

Mordecai Hamm to speak. To this crusade, a sixteen-year-old young man was invited. And at one of these meetings, Billy Graham received Christ. In 1972, Billy Graham was in Dallas, Texas, speaking to a group of Campus Crusade for Christ young people, and there he issued a bold challenge. He asked if there were any in the room who would give their lives to the gospel of Jesus Christ. A young nineteen-year-old man stood up and responded.

That was me, and my life has never been the same.

Never underestimate the power of one invitation.

Several years ago, I hired a landscape company to do some work on our family farm in Oregon. I was impressed with the two main workers, who labored diligently. I ended up conversing with one of them, whose name was Tim. He soon informed me that his name was spelled with a *y* instead of an *i*. I had never met a person whose name was spelled T-y-m, but it did make an impression on me that day.

> **Never underestimate the power of one invitation.**

The following week, Tym said, "Hey, my boss told me about you. You're on the radio."

"Yeah, I talk on the radio sometimes." I didn't say anything more.

The next week the landscaper came to our house again and said, "Hey, this past week I listened to you on the radio."

"Oh, good," I said. "I hope I said something beneficial." He chuckled. "Yep."

This went on over the next two and a half years. We had short regular conversations. None were terribly deep, but they developed into a friendship, and one day . . .

He passed by the door.

I got the chance to lead him to Christ, and now he's working at the New Hope Christian College in Eugene, Oregon, as our landscape designer and is walking with Christ. I owe much to this man who has become a friend and watches over the farm when I am in Hawaii or when I travel. I couldn't do what I do without him.

Tym is one reason why I stay near the door.

Let me tell you another reason.

When I moved to Oregon, I bought a horse. Then I thought, *My goodness, I don't know anything about horses.* So I decided to take my horse to a trainer. The woman who helped me purchase the horse introduced me to Tom, a lieutenant in the police department who also trains horses.

Tom not only trained my horse but taught me to do the same. We didn't talk about Christ, sin, or the church. Nope. We talked about horses. Tom was friendly, polite, and warm, and we spent many days training horses together as I learned the finer points of horses and riding.

A few weeks into our training, a friend asked Tom about what he does with his spare time. "Right now," he replied, "I'm training a guy named Wayne Cordeiro."

His friend said, "You mean the guy on the radio?"

"He's on the radio? For what?"

The next day at training, Tom told me that he had heard that I talk on the radio. I quipped, "Well, they don't have much else to play so they put me on."

"What do you talk about?"

I shared with him for about sixty seconds, and he said, "Oh, okay." That was it.

A week went by, and he came to me again and said, "I heard you write books. What have you written about?" I gave him a couple of books, and to my surprise, he read them.

He was near the door.

I eventually had the privilege of leading Tom and his dear wife to Christ. He's been attending church, walking with Christ, and doing fabulously. He now serves with New Hope International

Ministries as our Director of Operations. We have become the best of friends, and of course, we ride horses together.

But I still stay near the door. That's where I find Jesus hanging out a lot.

> I am the door of the sheep. If anyone enters through Me, he will be saved, and will go in and out and find pasture.
>
> Jesus (see John 10:7, 9)

Questions for individual reflection or group discussion:

1. What does it mean to "stay near the door"?

2. Can you identify some forgotten people in your community who are precious to Jesus? What about a maintenance person or a custodian? Will you spend a few minutes with them to nudge them closer to the door?

3. Never underestimate the power of one invitation. Share how you were invited to know Christ with the group.

4. Start a prayer list and record four names of people whom you will pray for. Regularly pray that they will one day come to Christ.

CHAPTER 8

INTERNAL CORRECTIONS

Let not steadfast love and faithfulness forsake you; bind them around your neck; write them on the tablet of your heart.

Proverbs 3:3 ESV

Two weeks before moving back to Hawaii, I realized I was soon about to live in the Mecca of bogeys, back nines, and bunkers. So I quickly found a professional golf instructor and asked him to teach me everything he knew.

He laughed. "Well, I can't teach you to be a professional golfer in this short amount of time," he said. "But I can show you what a correct golf swing looks like. After that, the key to greatness in golf is to keep practicing the basic swing, over and over again."

"Why is the basic swing so important?" I asked.

"Because right now you have no correct picture of what you should do," said the golf pro. "And without that correct picture, nothing else will fall into place. If you hit a ball well once, you won't know why you did it, and you won't be able to repeat it. Similarly, if you hit a bad shot, you won't know why it went bad, and you won't know how to correct it."

So every day for two weeks, that's what we worked on—the basic swing. Hour after hour, the golf pro instilled in me the mechanics of the fundamentals. We didn't work on anything else—not driving for distance, or putting, or getting out of the rough, or even the right way to drive a golf cart!

In hindsight, I know that those two weeks were the best golf lessons I could ever have. By learning that basic swing, I learned the foundation to being a great golfer. I learned what it looks like—and feels like—to have a correct basic swing.

It's a principle I've applied to other areas of life. Work on the foundation first. Develop a correct image of how things should be. Then you'll be able to navigate life's hazards and stay on the fairway.

Everything Made New

When it comes to following Christ purely and simply, we need to develop a correct picture of what a righteous heart looks like. Our conscience dwells in our heart of hearts, where we find the repository of our motives.

Everything in our inner being—our heart—must be aligned with the Word of God and the Spirit of Christ. Otherwise, if—and when—we get off course, we'll correct back to a faulty or worldly image. If we don't have a correct picture in place, we can be convinced we're right when we're dead wrong. Or worse, it would be like playing a prank on a friend by switching the cover picture of a jigsaw puzzle with another puzzle, then watching them struggle to match them up. In the same way, you can almost hear the adversary insidiously giggling while we are forcing the pieces to fit a false image.

Solomon could have been a golf pro of the soul. He corrects back with these words from Proverbs 3:3 (NASB):

> Do not let kindness and truth leave you;
> Bind them around your neck,
> Write them on the tablet of your heart.

That's basic to finding our way back. Take the foundations of kindness and truth and wrap them around your inner being. Let your heart be saturated with truth so that it becomes closely aligned with the truths of the Bible. Get the basic swing of your heart down correctly, and everything else will fall into place. When we get lost, we can find our way back.

Someone might be saying, "Wayne—hang on. You're telling us to have truthful hearts. How can our hearts ever be full of truth? A heart is evil!"

Yes, it's true that the Bible tells us that our hearts are desperately wicked (Jeremiah 17:9 NKJV). Yet it is equally important to note that the description of an evil heart fits an unregenerate person, someone who does not know and follow Christ. When a person knows, loves, and obeys Jesus, a new heart is given to that person. The old is wiped away. All things become new—even evil hearts. Ezekiel 36:26–27 (NKJV) describes this process:

> I will give you a new heart and put a new spirit within you; I will take the heart of stone out of your flesh and give you a heart of flesh. I will put My Spirit within you and cause you to walk in My statutes, and you will keep My judgments and do them.

That's the key. When the Spirit of God is put within us, we are able to walk in the pathways of God's statutes. By Christ's grace, everything is made new. Paul undergirds this teaching in 2 Corinthians 5:17 (NKJV):

If anyone is in Christ, he is a new creation; old things have passed away; behold, all things have become new.

As we draw close to Jesus, the core of our hearts and the practices that flow from our hearts become places of solidity and steadfastness. Our hearts become foundations for righteous living developed in conjunction with God and His Word.

Matching Outside Behavior to Inner Image

How do we develop this image of a righteous heart?

Paul describes the process in simple terms:

My children, . . . Christ [shall be] formed in you.

Galatians 4:19

Think about that—Christ is formed in us. The word *form* means a transformation takes place—one thing becomes something else. So when Christ is formed in us, it means that every believer can imitate the ideals of the Messiah. It also means that the Messiah lives through every believer.

Hebrews 5:14 describes how Christ is formed in us—by practice:

But solid food is for the mature, who because of practice have their senses trained to discern good and evil.

Let's say you're a tennis player. You have a picture in your mind's eye about what a perfect serve across the net should look like. The reality of your serve might be different than what you have in your head. But by practice you can continually match your outer practice with the inner picture.

That's the key. Keep practicing your serve until your outer motion matches the inner form in your mind. When you hit that tennis ball a thousand times according to the picture you have in your head, then the practice on the outside begins to match the ideal on the inside. You begin hitting the tennis ball over the net right at the far corner of the square on the other side—not just one out of ten times, but eight or nine out of ten.

The challenge is to get the correct form inside, then align the outside to that. Picture it now. You can close your eyes and see the perfect form of a professional tennis player, the arch of the back, the toss of the ball, the follow-through, the top spin. You try it once. You try it again. Each time you try it, you become more and more conformed to the ideal image. You don't change your inner form to match your outside behavior. You change your outside behavior to match your inner form.

Do you see how that applies to our hearts? Paul exhorts us to labor until we get that true picture of Christ. Then as Hebrews says, we practice until we train our senses. We begin to move into the process the more we do it.

Know what your heart needs to looks like, then keep matching your outer life to your inner life. Get the inside right and the outside will follow.

People of the Lie

Some years back the late author and psychiatrist M. Scott Peck wrote a book called *People of the Lie* in which he presented a historical case study about the horrific My Lai Massacre during the Vietnam War. Peck remains a controversial figure today, and, to be clear, I do not endorse the entirety of his work. Rather, I want to illustrate here what it looks like to be honest (or dishonest) on the inside.

During the war, a certain company of American soldiers suffered various attacks. Their orders were to go into a tiny Vietnamese village under the assumption that all innocent civilians would have left the area by a certain time of the day. Whoever remained would be enemies or enemy sympathizers.

The company went in with this assumption. But the assumption turned out to be false. Not all innocent civilians had left. Enemies were mixed in with the civilians. In the end, hundreds of Vietnamese people were killed with automatic weapons and the village was burned. Included with the dead soldiers were innocent women, children, and the elderly.

Peck interviewed some of the American soldiers involved in the atrocity and asked them why they would wipe out a village in this manner. The common answer given was that they couldn't take any chances. Even the children might have bombs strapped to them. In other words, they were simply following the orders of their commander.

Peck found that the commander had previously surveyed the situation, made a decision, and then ordered his men accordingly. Hindsight would show that because the commander had an inaccurate picture in his mind about the reality of the situation, he and his men did things they would not have normally done.

Here's my point: When a picture of reality is distorted, people can become deceived and act according to that deception.

Similarly, when our image of God is wrong, we can also become people who are deceived and act in harmful ways.

Let's look at the practical applications of this more closely. Wrong images of God include the following:

- *God loves us and everything we do, so he is a lenient God. Therefore we can live in immorality.*
- *God is legalistic and loves to punish us. God is always angry with us.*
- *God is the giver of good gifts, so He wants us to live in continual luxury with opulence and excess.*

If we are living with any of these faulty images in mind, then we, too, can become people of the lie. Our behavior will reflect the faulty image that is in our hearts.

When we correct back to the image of God in Scripture, we can see that these images of God are faulty, and we can adjust accordingly and live in righteousness.

> "It is impossible for a man to learn what he thinks he already knows."
> Epictetus

The voice of God, the foundation of truth, will always sound just like the Bible. Do you want to know what God is like? Read the Bible. That gives you a true picture of Christ.

The question then becomes *Do we have the correct picture of God in our hearts?* We must have a correct biblical picture of God. Once that picture is in place, we need to get our outer practice to match our inner picture. But be sure to allow the Word of God to give you the correct picture of Jesus.

He is kind but not necessarily tolerant.

He is forbearing but not soft.

He is all-powerful but not all-controlling.

He is fatherly, but not patronizing.

He is patient, but not lenient.

Four Hundred Flying Hours

Some time ago a rash of flying accidents occurred across North America. When the Federal Aviation Administration (FAA) began to investigate, they found that most of the accidents were taking place with pilots who had around 400 flying hours. Apparently, the findings concluded, these pilots assumed that because they already had a lot of hours under their belts, they didn't need to check their planes out as carefully. Or they knew the planes, so they'd compromise and cut corners with inspections.

By contrast, beginning pilots with fewer hours were extremely careful, even painstaking in their preflight routines, meticulously inspecting every rivet of the airplane.

The long-flying veterans with more than 400 hours of flight time were just as meticulous. They did it by the book.

But the pilots in the middle, those with around 400 flying hours, were the most accident prone.

Sometimes we as Christians are 400-flying-hour disciples. Accidents take place because we stop doing it by the Book. We stop studying the Word of God. We compromise on devotions. We fail to embrace His ordinances, and we slip up on the rules. We slump on allowing the standards of Scripture and the Holy Spirit to inspect every "rivet" in our hearts and lives. We go on day after day cutting corners, wondering why we lose power on the climbs, and we stall. Accidents may often be the consequences of thinking we know better.

It's time that we correct back to Jesus.

Command Central

Proverbs says to guard our hearts with all diligence (4:23). Our hearts are the control room of the rest of our lives. If there's something wrong in our control room, everything else suffers.

For several years I was a chaplain at a jail in Oregon. It was a modern facility with electronic door locks, each operated by a central office in the heart of the structure.

The first time I went to the jail for a chapel service, I didn't know what to expect. I remember approaching the first door, pressing a button, and hearing an anonymous voice over a hidden speaker: "Show your ID to the camera, please." So I took out my driver's license and presented it before a lens protruding from the exterior wall.

"Your purpose here?" the voice asked.

"I'm a chaplain," I replied (looking for a direction into which I should be speaking). "I'm holding a service in the chapel today for the inmates."

"Okay," said the voice. "*Just follow the opening doors.*"

I heard a loud *click,* and the door directly in front of me swung open. I proceeded through it until I came to the end of a narrow hallway with a door that magically opened as I approached. Down a second hallway, I found an elevator. I paused, and almost on cue, the metal door separated and I entered. Wondering which level the chapel was on, I searched for buttons that might guide me to the right floor. There were no buttons on the elevator. I was stumped. In front of me, the doors slowly closed. After a few rings, the doors again opened, and I found myself at the entrance to the chapel.

A voice behind me courteously said, "Thank you. Have a nice service."

When the service was over, one of the deputies invited me on a quick tour. I was so intrigued by the whole experience that I readily agreed. He ushered me down to the central control room. Cameras had been placed throughout the jail and screens in the control room displayed every movement made in the facility. The central room controlled the whole building—every door, every light, every entry, and every exit.

"How interesting," I thought. "Get the wrong guy in here and he could release every inmate or shut out every officer." This made the control room an incredibly strategic location.

Our heart is that control room. Let in wrong thoughts or give over control to destructive personalities, and we would, in short order, be in dire straits.

It's time to let Jesus in.

Scrub Your Heart Often

Do you want Christ to run your control room? Scripture exhorts us to keep our minds focused on things above (Colossians 3:1–2).

Part of that means continually going back to the question "Is my heart right?" In other words—is my inner being grounded and centered where it needs to be, on God's truth?

Sometimes I stop by the ocean near my office in Hawaii, sit on a brick wall, and simply talk to the Lord. In prayer I'll ask God to reveal any area that needs refining. I'll go through the various rooms in my heart to see if they're aligned with things above. Questions include: *God, how's my marriage doing? How's my devotional life going? Am I being grateful? How am I doing in my attitude toward people who give me problems?*

It's important to do this often. If I sense my heart is not centered on God's truth, I'll take steps to correct it. Daily troubles and concerns can easily knock us off track.

Right now, for instance, a man is giving me some trouble at the church, and I need to consciously monitor my heart to make sure my attitude is right toward him.

The trouble began when the mayor asked me to give an invocation at a Christmas event that was held at an outdoor venue on government property. I prayed for the city. During my prayer, an antagonistic atheistic startled the crowd. His booming voice caught us all off guard.

"Violation!" he yelled. "I object! Separation of church and state!" I hesitated for a moment after his contradictory intrusion, but with all the concentration I could muster, I continued with my prayer of blessing. His heckling continued through to the final *Amen.*

But the evening's activist was not satisfied with his rudeness. Soon afterward, he went to the school where we hold our services, contacted officials, and insisted on investigating all our rental contracts. He inspected every event, searching for the smallest violation, and then filed complaints with the Education Department, demanding repercussions.

He continued battering us to the point where we began to search for a good attorney.

I was upset, but I remembered the words of Paul, "Be angry, and yet do not sin. Do not let the sun go down on your anger" (Ephesians 4:26). I needed to ask God, "How am I doing with my anger?"

I also realize that I cannot be gullible, nor is it responsible to roll over and play dead. I'm not going to let one person's noise cause me to shut down my faith in public, and I'm not going to go into hiding. But neither am I going to couch my revenge in spiritual eloquence. So I needed to shut myself in with God and get His advice.

That's the key: Ask God about everything. How did Jesus deal with His detractors? How did He deal with those who were persecuting Him?

I need to scrub my heart, and not only scrub it, but get Wayne out of it, so that Jesus is opening and closing the doors in the control room.

Getting back to Jesus. That's what this book is all about.

> Examine yourselves to see whether you are in the faith; test yourselves. Do you not realize that Christ Jesus is in you—unless, of course, you fail the test?
>
> 2 Corinthians 13:5 NIV

Keeping Short Accounts

The other day I circumvented one of my staff leader's decisions. In other words, I micromanaged him. He was gracious and didn't say anything, but a day later I was asking the Lord, "God, how am I doing as a leader with respect to my staff?" The Holy Spirit brought this incident to my mind. I knew I needed to talk to this man and ask for his forgiveness. So I did. Forgiveness was asked for and received. The relationship was restored, and we moved forward. This wasn't the first time I've done something like this. Not by far. I've long since learned that when sin remains unconfessed it acts as a burr caught in my soul.

The mature believer will want to initiate the process himself. But if we don't take the initiative to confess sin, the Holy Spirit will take it for us. There are three stages of spiritual health. Stage 1 is the most immature. Stage 3 is the most mature. The goal is to move toward continually operating in stage 3.

- In stage 1, the Holy Spirit convicts us of sin via an outside party; then we confess our sin to God. God uses a spiritual supervisor such as a spouse or accountability partner to draw attention to our sin. In stage 1, the temptation is to give excuses. But the goal is to agree with God and admit the wrongdoing.
- In stage 2, the Holy Spirit illuminates a problem to us directly, and then we confess it. Our conscience feels a twinge and we respond.
- In stage 3, we self-correct. We ask the Holy Spirit to search our hearts, find sin, and then we confess it. In this stage we initiate, we ask, we stop by the ocean to talk with God. And God responds. He shows us a sin polyp. It's something that's precancerous—dangerous but not yet deadly. Stage 3 is the goal.

The wise Christian self-corrects. I say this to leaders: If you have staff and employees who know how to self-correct, they're as precious as gold. David employed this same means.

> Search me, God, and know my heart;
> test me and know my anxious thoughts.
> See if there is any offensive way in me,
> and lead me in the way everlasting.
> Psalm 139:23–24 NIV

Any training process works this way.

The Ultimate Goal

I love working with horses. I have three of them. When I train these magnificent creatures, my goal is not to control them. Ultimately it's that they learn to correct themselves.

Here's an example:

The day's teaching begins with a lesson called "following the fence." I begin by setting them to follow a fence line on a two-acre paddock. I make sure that their reins are not too tight so as to micromanage their every move. Instead, I give them a loose rein and then let them move forward. Should they stray several feet from the fence line, I don't pull on the reins. In my mind, I draw an imaginary line parallel to the fence about four feet away, and I wait until they cross that line. Should they violate my imaginary border, I will immediately steer them back to the fence line. If they wander two or three feet without crossing that imaginary line, I let them wander. But as soon as they meander beyond the invisible boundary, the immediate schooling begins. Soon they will discover that the best place for their peace of mind is right along the fence line.

The best horse is one that has learned to self-correct.

God works the same way with us. His ultimate desire is not to put us on a tight rein. He wants us to discern the correct boundaries for living and for relationships, and to follow Him by experience and wisdom, not by coercion and whip.

Here's one of the best prayers you can pray: "Lord, as soon as I cross any line that I shouldn't, would you please school me back immediately? Don't let me stray a foot or two past it; even at one centimeter, even though unintentional, would you please intervene? I'm not asking for a tight rein. Instead, I am asking for a sensitive heart."

More detrimental than what I do is what I *tolerate*. Although I want to avoid the slips, should I err, I can repent. However, if I begin to tolerate error, I will be duped into thinking that repentance is not necessary. That's when deception sets down its roots.

It's not what a leader or a parent does that can be most detrimental. It is what a leader or parent *tolerates.*

Ducks and Pumpkins

The story is told of a certain African tribe that learned an easy way to capture ducks in a river. Catching their agile and wary dinner would be a feat indeed, so they formulated a plan.

The tribesmen learned to go upstream, place a pumpkin in the river, and let it slowly float down into the flock of ducks. At first, the cautious fowl would quack and fly away. After all, it wasn't ordinary for *pumpkins* to float down the river! But the persistent tribesmen would subsequently float another pumpkin into the re-gathered ducks. Again they would scatter, only to return after the strange sphere had passed. Again, the hungry hunters would float another pumpkin. This time the ducks would remain, with a cautious eye on the pumpkin, and with each successive passing, the ducks would become more comfortable, until they finally accepted the pumpkins as a normal part of life.

When the natives saw that the pumpkins no longer bothered the ducks, they hollowed out pumpkins, put them over their heads, and walked into the river. Meandering into the midst of the tolerant fowl, they pulled them down one at a time.

Dinner?

Roast duck.

If we don't correct our hearts back to Jesus, it won't be long until we start tolerating "pumpkins." They have a seductive way of sneaking in to our marriages, our thinking, our language, and our theology. They creep in one by one until we sink beneath them and enter a watery grave.

Sin seldom starts out with evil intent. It often begins with clean hearts and good intent—an innocent lunch with a co-worker whose marriage is struggling or a harmless travel excursion for business purposes that grows until we are caught in a web of emotion. As our tolerance levels rise incrementally we cross the invisible line that runs parallel to the fence with increasing frequency until it no longer causes any concern.

My friends, if Jesus isn't allowed to cleanse our hearts, sinful habits that are repeated aren't as bothersome anymore. The first time we do something wrong, our conscience stings. The second time, it concerns us. The third time, it informs us. By the fourth time, we don't notice the breach, and with each successive infringement, we begin to endorse the action as the new normal.

Learn to self-correct.

Notice pumpkins.

Draw near to Jesus, and He will draw near to you.

Questions for individual reflection or group discussion:

1. Why is it so important to develop a core of truth in our hearts?

2. Reread Galatians 4:19. What does it mean when it says, "Christ [shall be] formed in you"?

3. What practical ways can you train your senses "to discern good and evil" (Hebrews 5:14)?

4. What are some faulty concepts of God that people have, and how will those concepts affect how they live?

5. What are some characteristics of God that we learn of in His Word, and how will these characteristics affect how we live?

CHAPTER 9

THE POWER OF CONTENTMENT

Now when the queen of Sheba heard of the fame of Solomon concerning the name of the Lord, she came to test him with hard questions.

1 Kings 10:1 ESV

I sometimes test myself with hard questions. I might be a bit unusual, but I drill myself like someone with flash cards before an exam. I guess it's because I believe that I need to know the hard answers before the hard questions are asked.

And they will be asked!

Some people don't fall into sin only because they've not had the opportunity yet. But those opportunities will come, and when they do, trying to figure out an escape will be futile. I have to know the answers before the temptations are tugging at my soul, and those questions will come at my lowest point.

131

So I wait for a time when I am close to God and in a healthy frame of mind, and I write down what I believe is my assignment and what my life is to be about. I ask myself the hard questions and then answer them. I write these down and keep them close. The reason?

There will be a time when I will NOT feel close to God and when I am NOT in a healthy frame of mind, and that's when the enemy comes to do his bidding. At that time the questions will sound more rational than ever before and most alluring:

- Wouldn't you like to be in a healthier relationship with someone other than your spouse? Don't you deserve a person who's more satisfying?
- You are worth much more than what they pay you. You deserve a salary much more rewarding than what you are getting.

The queen tested Solomon with difficult questions. She had good motives, examining him to see if what she had heard about him was true. Solomon's wisdom shone through as he exceeded her expectations. Those hard questions didn't take Solomon by surprise. He had thought them through beforehand; they were answered in his mind before they were asked.

Hard questions.

It's not a matter of *if*, but *when,* and those questions won't only come from well-meaning queens. As we find in Luke 4, the archenemy of our souls is asking hard questions—with a hook.

In Luke 4:1–13, the devil used his most devious strategy to tempt the Son of God when He was at His lowest. You've got to bring your A game if you want to tempt the Creator of the universe, and he did.

Jesus, full of the Holy Spirit, returned from the Jordan and was led around by the Spirit in the wilderness for forty days, being tempted by the devil. And He ate nothing during those days, and when they had ended, He became hungry.

Luke 4:1–3

Are you familiar with the story? The devil said to the Son of God, "So, you've been fasting for forty days. Hungry? Turn these stones into bread." In other words, "Why don't you use your authority on yourself for once. You're hungry! Use your powers to feed yourself! You need to provide for yourself!"

He then showed Him in an instant all the kingdoms of the world. "You could do more if you had prominence and affluence. It is mine to give. Trade in what you have for success. After all, isn't that everyone's goal in life? Imagine what you want, and whatever your mind can conceive, I can deliver."

The third time, he ushered Jesus to the pinnacle of the temple and said, "Throw yourself down. Angels will catch you. After all, isn't it written that God will give His angels charge over you to keep you from harm?" Satan quoted Psalm 91:11–12. The devil memorized enough Scripture to distort it for his purposes. He's a master at using the Word for his gain, and the temptation is for us to do the same.

But the bottom line is this: He wanted to find where Jesus may be dissatisfied because that would signal where He was most vulnerable.

Dissatisfaction

In all three of the temptations, the overarching theme was to locate where Jesus may be discontent, and that would determine the archenemy's starting point. The devil was saying, "Look—if you're God, then why are you still hungry? Why are you still poor? If God loves you, then why do you have nothing? You have no house, no place to lay your head, and you surely have no prominence. How dissatisfying!"

Your Enemy's Big Goal

In 1965 a hit song came out that's still played on classic radio stations today: "I Can't Get No Satisfaction." It became one of the top hits of all time.

It's almost prophetic.

Dissatisfaction is a universal feeling no matter what the generation. The devil uses dissatisfaction to its fullest capacity, and if he can succeed at making us feel discontent and disgruntled, we will play right into his hands.

This is the same temptation he used in the Garden. The devil came in the form of a serpent to Eve. She could eat any fruit in the whole Garden—except one.

Why do you think God put one limitation on Adam and Eve? He did it because He wanted them to have a choice. Without it, they would be like robots. With one limitation in place, they were given the option to obey or to not obey.

> **If the enemy can succeed at making us feel discontent and disgruntled, we will play right into his hands.**

So, the serpent hissed, "Eve, what about that fruit? Are you allowed to eat it?"

"No," Eve said. "God said we could eat anything except that."

The devil hissed again. "Isn't that *dissatisfying*? Don't you feel like a slave without freedom? You don't need others telling you what's right or wrong for you. If it's wrong for them, fine. You are a big girl and you can decide for yourself. You don't need God to tell you what you should or should not do."

Eve considered his reasoning. It sounded rational!

"You know, you're right! Why can't I do what I want to do?! I can decide for myself what is right and what is wrong!"

She took the forbidden fruit and ate it, and also gave some to her husband, and he ate it. So began the downfall of mankind. (See Genesis 3:1–6.)

Dissatisfaction—it's an age-old weapon.

It's not rocket science. It's very workable. The devil's bottom line to tempt you and me is to get us to feel dissatisfied with who we are and what we have.

- Disappointed with our marriage.
- Discontented with our salary.
- Bored with our church.
- Dissatisfied with our car.
- Displeased with our house.
- Dissatisfied with our faith.

Whenever a lack of satisfaction seeps into our lives, we're on very dangerous ground. Our eyes get distracted and we become a host to other spiritual parasites:

- We get secretly jealous.
- We start to covet what others have.
- We become susceptible to advertising for something better.
- We compare ourselves with others.
- We complain about those who have more.
- We grumble about what we should have but don't.

It's time to get back to Jesus!

More Common Than You Think

Now the people became like those who complain of adversity.

Numbers 11:1

It started long ago. They had manna, the protection of the Lord, His presence, a great earthly leader, and no worries about the

135

pursuing Pharaoh and his army. They were chilling somewhere on the other side of the Red Sea.

But still they weren't satisfied. They began to complain like those who were in adversity even though, in reality, they were not. That's how it works, doesn't it? We *feel like* we are in dire straits when we are not. But if we think we are trapped or that we are in a situation that cannot be resolved, then the adversary gets us to make foolish decisions. The result?

We make a permanent decision based on a temporary setback.

That's what suicide is. A permanent decision based on a temporary setback. So is divorce, or quitting something in frustration (and having your future adversely affected).

Dissatisfaction can be a ruse and a deception. It spawns fear. What is fear? Using the letters of that word might help us to remember:

False
Evidence
Appearing
Real

The Ruse of Dissatisfaction

Once there was a customer who was always dissatisfied. He went to a restaurant, ordered a sandwich, and became irate—not at the sandwich, but at the temperature inside the restaurant. He called the waiter over and said, "It is just too hot in here. Can't you do something about the heat?!"

"Sure," the waiter said. "We'll get that taken care of right away, sir."

The waiter disappeared to the back room, then returned. "How's that, sir?"

"Better, better."

A little while later the customer said, "Now it's too cold! Can't you turn down your air-conditioner?"

"Absolutely, sir," the waiter said. "I'll be right back." Again he disappeared and came back. "Is that any better?"

"We will see. We will see."

After a while the customer said, "Excuse me! Now it's getting warm again."

The waiter said, "Let me go back and check." Once again he went to the back room. "How's that, sir?"

"Better."

In a few minutes, the dissatisfied customer got up, paid his bill, and left.

Another customer had been watching the scene unfold. He called to the waiter and said, "May I commend you? You are the most tolerant person I have ever seen. I would have punched that guy in the jaw long ago. But instead you just calmly went back each time and adjusted the air-conditioner."

"Well, actually," said the waiter. "I'll let you in on a little secret."

"What's that?"

"We don't have air-conditioning in here."

Normalizing the Abnormal

Dissatisfaction is all around us, but we've grown so accustomed to it that we seldom realize it. With every advertisement we see, we are told we need to be dissatisfied.

- If you have last year's model of phone . . . you should be dissatisfied.
- If your clothes are not the right brand . . . you need to be dissatisfied.
- If your car is out of date . . . you should be dissatisfied.

- If you're not making as much as the other guy . . . you should be dissatisfied.
- If your church doesn't have as nice a facility as the one down the street . . . you should be dissatisfied.

The more dissatisfied we are the more Madison Avenue marketers can sell us. Over time we find that nothing is good enough if it isn't new, instant, trendy, or convenient. Dissatisfaction permeates our lives. The more we're dissatisfied, the more it takes over. We find we're no longer simply dissatisfied with our phones, clothes, cars, and pizza, but we're also dissatisfied with our friends, churches, ministries, spouses, children—and God.

Jesus models contentment for us. The Pharisees were plotting to kill Him. He was chased down by the demon possessed, followed after by lepers, slept outdoors, and was rejected by His followers.

Yet He refused to be dissatisfied or disheartened.

You could hear it in His voice when the disciples were in the boat with Him. He had a rough day dodging the demons and answering the Pharisees. They got into a boat and rowed right into a storm. But Jesus had fallen asleep. The disciples panicked and roused Him from His slumber with the words "Don't you care that we are perishing!?"

Jesus rebuked the winds and the sea became calm. He turned to His disciples and said, "Why are you afraid? Do you still have no faith?" (Mark 4:40).

Notice the words *"No faith."*

Dissatisfaction is a symptom of disappointment with how God is caring for us.

Satisfaction With God

The psalmist David hit it on the nose when he wrote:

The lines have fallen to me in pleasant places; indeed my heritage is beautiful to me.

Psalm 16:6

Picture the old game of pickup sticks. When dropped on a tabletop, the thin sticks fall into disarray. The object of the game is to pick up each stick without moving any other.

Sometimes our lives may resemble a pile of pickup sticks, a cluttered mess of unorganized pieces going every which way. But we can choose to say, like David did, "No matter how my life might look right now, no matter how clumped or disordered, no matter how hectic or tangled, I am satisfied with the way God is treating me at this time in my life."

The lines have fallen to me in pleasant places.

Be Careful What You Wish For

Do not be hasty in word or impulsive in thought to bring up a matter in the presence of God. For God is in heaven and you are on the earth; therefore let your words be few.

Ecclesiastes 5:2

Solomon offers wise counsel. God sees things from the 32,000-foot level while we see things up close. And what makes matters worse is discontentment. It skews our decision-making. We trade long-lasting peace for temporary comfort as we humorously find in the following story:

A man and his wife, both sixty-five years old, took a vacation to the Bahamas to celebrate their retirement. One day while walking on the beach, they found a lamp stuck in the sand. They picked it up, dusted it off, and *"Whoosh!"* Out popped a genie!

"As a reward for releasing me from this bottle after being cooped up here for 100 years, I will grant each of you one wish," the genie said.

"Oh, this is wonderful!" the wife said. "My wish is to own a beautiful cabana by the ocean where we can spend the rest of our retirement."

"Your wish is my command," said the genie. All of a sudden a beautiful oceanfront cabana appeared complete with waiters, palm trees, and buffet tables of gourmet food.

"Okay, you're next," said the genie to the husband.

The husband gazed at the scantily clad women in bikinis on the beach, then looked at his own wife and blurted, "I want to be married to a wife thirty years younger!"

"Your wish is my command," said the genie.

Poof! Immediately, he was ninety-five years old.

Be careful what you yearn for. Discontentment can change your future for the worse!

One man said, "There are two sorrows in life. One is when you don't get what you crave, and the other is when you get it."

We might wish for a big fancy house, but when we get it we find that we're overwhelmed by the monthly mortgage payments. Or we might long for a different spouse, but then we get divorced and marry someone else, and find out that this relationship is just as flawed and challenging as the first.

It's so easy to be dissatisfied with what we have. When the enemy is successful in creating dissatisfaction within us, then we begin to make unwise decisions.

What's the solution? How can we combat dissatisfaction? Here's the thing about any temptation: We can't prepare for it after it hits us. We must prepare well in advance.

Some years ago I was in Sri Lanka when a tsunami hit. Complete areas were wiped out because buildings were built right on the ground with no foundations.

But as we drove through the wreckage along the shore I noticed a hotel. The hotel's siding and roof were damaged, but the building was still structurally sound and stood tall. In fact, its location was by the ocean right in the path of the tsunami. But it was still standing. Why?

We looked under the hotel and could see strong pilings that had been driven 100 feet into the depths of the earth. Those pilings were set securely in place long before the tsunami ever hit the placid shores.

If a tsunami is coming, can you imagine hurriedly trying to drive a piling into the ground? It would be far too late. The same is true for us. When the enemy comes and tries to get us to feel dissatisfied, if we do not already have pilings driven deeply in our life, we will fall.

How do we create a solid foundation that combats dissatisfaction?

The Piling of Gratefulness

Gratefulness is a piling that needs to be driven early on. It does not come automatically, and it does not come easily. Isn't it true that when you give a gift to kids, they grab it and leave? I remember my mother yanking me back by my hair once and firmly saying under her breath, "You say, 'Thank you!'"

"Thank you," I said. And then she let me have my hair back.

But even adults fall into the trap of ungratefulness.

> In everything give thanks; for this is God's will for you in Christ Jesus.
>
> 1 Thessalonians 5:18

What is God's will for us? Very simply: Give thanks in everything.

You might wonder how to be grateful when problems come. Perhaps your wallet got stolen. Are you to be thankful for evil? No—God himself is not thankful for evil, and God's invitation always is to agree with Him. But the key is to be thankful *through* every situation, or *in the midst* of anything. If we belong to Christ, nothing touches our lives unless it has already gone over His desk and He has said, "OK."

God sees the big picture of all circumstances that come our way, and He has promised,

> God causes all things to work together for good to those who love God, to those who are called according to His purpose.
>
> Romans 8:28

In everything give thanks—that's how a foundation of gratefulness is created. Giving thanks will protect our spirits. It will safeguard our souls from blaming God, becoming bitter, and turning rancid.

Gratefulness is something every single one of us can have.

Gratefulness is something every single one of us can have. It's a critical piling that must be driven deep early on. Don't wait until there's something spectacular to be grateful about. Don't wait to win the lottery, to come in first, receive a promotion, or get an award.

Drive deep the pilings of gratefulness first or be vulnerable to the changing tides that come your way. We must learn to be grateful no matter what our circumstances.

The Piling of Contentment

Surprisingly, we do not need a drawer full of bling or a bank account of millions in order to be content.

> If we have food and covering, with these we shall be content.
>
> 1 Timothy 6:8

How many of us have eaten today? How many of us are clothed? The Bible says if we have eaten something today and are clothed, that's enough to be content.

But we always seem to think there's one more thing we need before we'll be content:

- "If I finish college, I will be satisfied!"
- "When I marry the man of my dreams, I will be happy."
- "When I get my career going, I will be fulfilled."
- "When my bills are paid, I'll be content."

Dream on.

When you find yourself always wanting more, get ready. The adversary of your soul has a rather large wave on its way. You are being set up.

My wife, Anna, and I have developed a habit that started many years ago when we were first married and bought our first house for $19,300. It was 720 square feet. That is about as big as a normal living room and dining room today, but back then it was the whole house.

I remember coming home one evening and saying, "Isn't this beautiful, Anna? Isn't this a great house?" We had a small couch and one end table we had displaced from the bedroom. But on it my wife had put a handful of flowers in a simple vase.

She looked around and said, "But it's so small."

"Well, a small house is OK. You can just turn around with a broom and clean the whole house! You can wipe the walls while standing in one place! We can go from room to room with only a few steps!"

She laughed. "Yes, I guess those are good features," she said.

"And just think of all the money we'll save on utilities!"

We both laughed.

"Don't we have a nice house? It's just right, and we're content!"

She caught the vision, and from then on we both started regularly affirming what the Lord had provided. It became a common saying between us—"Don't we have a great house?"

What were we doing? We were intentionally driving deep the pilings of gratefulness and contentment before any tsunamis hit.

Today, after being married for more than thirty-eight years, we've got a beautiful house on a ranch in Oregon as well as a smaller condo in Hawaii, and we're content. But we didn't begin there. We began with what we had—even when we had very little. It was the heart that needed to increase long before our possessions did. Otherwise when our possessions increased, so would our dependency on them.

Hindering Prayers

Being dissatisfied could cause our prayers to go unanswered. This is a principle that not many realize, but I hear it all the time. Let me explain.

"Dear God," we pray at a church membership meeting. "Please grow our little church!" He starts to answer our prayers, and now we complain that there's no parking.

"Dear God, bring sinners to our church!" you pray. Then God brings your neighbor that used to have eyes for your wife, and now you say, "Why doesn't he go to another church! I'll bet he's here because of my wife!"

We continue to pray, "Dear God, teach me how to be a servant!" Then when we are corrected, we figure it's time to leave the church and find another one that is "friendlier."

So after a time, God stops answering our prayers because when He does, we only complain. Practicing contentment may be one of the best ways to open the floodgates of answered prayer.

Off to the Dump

When I was a pastor in Hilo before coming to Honolulu, we were not making much. I prayed for ways to save on our monthly bills. One day, I noticed that we paid for rubbish service, and over the months it grew to be more and more expensive. After work one day, I said to my wife, "Honey, why don't I just buy an old pickup, and we can load our trash in it. Then when it fills up, I'll take it to the landfill. We can save $40 a month, plus we'll have a pickup for other uses." She agreed.

A week passed, and down the road I saw an old rusty brown pickup in the back of a neighbor's yard with a sign on it: "For Sale—$500."

What a price!

It was an ugly-looking thing, but it was perfect for hauling rubbish to the dump. Now, there were a few minor issues that we needed to be aware of.

First, if you opened the driver's door too far, it fell off the hinge, so you had to know a trick or two. When you got the driver's door opened 75 percent of the way, you quickly got in. There were other unique characteristics.

Two four-inch holes were rusted through the floorboards. I put a piece of cardboard over the holes to keep the water on the roads from intruding on our otherwise dry cab. You see, in Hilo it rains only twice a year—once from January through June, and the other from July through December.

But there were a few sunny days, so on those anomalies, I'd remove the cardboard to enjoy the white lines passing by beneath our feet when we changed lanes.

I remember the first time my wife got in. I said, "Isn't this a cool truck?"

She gave me a quizzical look. "Honey, I think you've been in this rain too long."

"No," I said, motioning to the floorboards. "Free air-conditioning!"

She laughed. "If we break down, we can be like the Flintstones and just run the car along with our legs."

You ask my kids today what was their favorite car to ride in, and they will tell you about that old pickup. It didn't have cruise control, leather seats, power windows, or a fancy sound system. It was just fun. We would go to the dump and get rid of the stuff and drive back home. The holes in the floorboard were cool because you could eat an apple and throw the core right through the bottom and no one would know you were littering.

Today we have a newer car and a larger home, but we couldn't wait for them before learning contentment. It starts when there's little to be content about. But isn't that just like Jesus?

> Practice the art of contentment, even if it doesn't seem like you have much to be grateful for.

Each of us will experience some hard times and lean years, but you'll come through them if you drive the pilings deep long before you need them.

Start now.

Practice the art of contentment, even if it doesn't seem like you have much to be grateful for. You have food and clothing.

Start there.

You will develop the spirit that combats dissatisfaction.

But watch out! If you are not developing the art of contentment, you will be just a hairsbreadth away from being dissatisfied with everything in life: your marriage, your looks, your hair, your clothes, your money, your church, your children, your extended family, your job. Whatever it might be, you'll always need more.

Gratefulness and contentment give you fresh eyes through which you see life.

- They can turn a rusty pickup into a thrilling Disneyland ride!
- They can transform an ordeal into an adventure.
- They make you look for the miracle rather than the consequence.
- They remind you that Jesus is all you need in the times when Jesus is all you got!

You just might be two pilings away from a fantastic life.

Train Your Eyes to See What Is Good!

What you look at is what you'll see. It's like looking for a used car that you'd like to purchase. Once you decide what kind of car that is, you'll find during the next week that everyone is driving that kind of car. Now, the same cars were there the week before, but you didn't see them. Why?

Practice looking for Jesus. You'll see Him everywhere.

Because you weren't looking for them.

- If you look for what's bad about your spouse, you'll find that you married a bad spouse!
- If you look for what is terrible about your situation, you'll see that you're in a heap of a mess.
- If you look for what's less than ideal about your car, you'll be dissatisfied with your wheels.

147

- If you compare your smartphone, or monthly payment plan, or interest rate, or breed of dog with someone else's, you'll want something more.
- If you look for bad news, you'll find it everywhere.
- If you look for blemishes, you'll discover them.

Instead, practice looking for Jesus. You'll see Him *everywhere.* Look for what's good and you'll find that the way God is treating you in this season of your life is the best ever, and even small houses and old pickups start to look good!

Questions for individual reflection or group discussion:

1. Why do you think we are so vulnerable to dissatisfaction?

2. Read Psalm 81:10–16. What did the Israelites need to do, and what was God's promise to them if they did it?

3. What do you think causes entitlement? Does discontentment play into this disease that afflicts so many people today?

4. In what ways can we protect ourselves from dissatisfaction?

5. What things should you be grateful for every day? Make a list that might include people, your faith, and your health.

CHAPTER 10

LIVING LIFE . . . ALONG THE WAY

Your ears will hear a word behind you, "This is the way, walk in it," whenever you turn to the right or to the left.

Isaiah 30:21

A while back I was scheduled to lead worship on a Wednesday night at our church. I hadn't played my guitar for a while, so I planned to spend Wednesday afternoon going through the songs. I didn't have much time to spend in practice, so I wanted to be as efficient with my time as possible. Instead of making the drive home, I stopped at a park to practice.

When I was finished practicing, I put my guitar back into the case and was about to rush off, when I saw a homeless man on the bench next to mine.

My first thought was to head back to my car. I had plenty of other important things to do. But I decided to be polite, so as I turned to go, I said in passing, "Hey, how are you doing?"

I really didn't want to know because I had a midweek service to do.

"Okay," he said. "You sounded good on the guitar. I'm just learning the ukulele. Want to play for a while together?"

My first thought again was to stay on task. I needed to get back to the church, plus I didn't want to play with a beginner. But I glanced at my watch and saw that I could spare a few minutes.

I took out my guitar, and we stumbled through a few songs. The man started grinning, and that got me to grinning, and the more we played, the more we both started to enjoy ourselves.

> We all will be busy from time to time, but we don't need to be hurried.

When the set was finished he asked, "What do you do?"

"I work for God," I said.

"You work for God . . . Wow! What a great job!" he said. "You think He knows about me?"

That began a great conversation about Jesus and about this man's life—nothing earth-shattering, but just enough to introduce the man to the love of Jesus.

The next week I went to the same park again. The man I played with wasn't there, but at the same bench sat another man.

"Hey, I remember you," he said. "You played guitar with Smitty on the ukulele."

"Oh," I said. "I never caught his name. Smitty, huh? Nice man."

"Do you know he died a few days ago?"

I was shocked. "He what? I was just with him!"

"Yeah. A massive heart attack. We'll all miss him here at the park."

It wasn't the midweek service that God had in mind. It was talking to Smitty about Jesus. Life happened along the way. . . .

Eternal life.

When we consider Jesus and the way of His discipleship, so many important acts happened *along the way*. Read the following excerpts and notice the life that takes place in between.

- In Mark 5:21–43, Jesus was on His way to the house of an important official, Jairus, to heal his ailing daughter. Yet in between, a woman with a hemorrhage touched His coat, and she was healed. Something eternal took place between points A and B.
- In Luke 17:11–19, ten lepers needed cleansing, and when Jesus saw them, He simply said, "Go and show yourselves to the priest." As they were heading over to the priest, the lepers were healed. A miracle happened *along the way* between points A and B.
- In John 4:1–42, Jesus was traveling from Galilee down to Jerusalem and stopped off at a town called Sychar in the region of Samaria. Along the way, Jesus met a woman while sitting at a well. For the first time ever, the woman encountered understanding, grace, forgiveness, and restoration. Something marvelous happened between points A and B.

What we think is our goal may be distinctly different from God's goal. Miss those in-between moments and we just might miss what's eternal.

The Watermelon Party

A while back I was set to meet with some well-known businessmen. I am usually quite punctual, but not that day. I arrived twenty minutes late.

One of the more direct individuals squared off with me as soon as I arrived.

"You're usually pretty early. What happened?"

"Well, actually," I said, "I'm late because I was playing with my granddaughter."

"What?" he replied. "Your granddaughter?"

I recounted what had transpired: "You see, my granddaughter loves watermelon, and just before I left for this meeting, she ran up to me and said, 'Papa, do you like watermelon?'"

"She calls me Papa," I whispered.

"I answered, 'I sure do, Katie.' She replied with a twinkle in her eye, 'Me too! Can I have some?' and I said, 'Sure.' So I went to our refrigerator and cut up a watermelon into bite-sized chunks, and just like that, we had ourselves a watermelon party. What a great moment."

One of the businessmen standing next to us turned to me and said. "You know, God just filled in an empty spot I've been carrying around for a couple weeks. He just spoke to me about what I need to do more of—spend time with my children . . . *eating watermelon*."

Some of the most eternal events in life happen along the way.

God's Goal or Ours?

A man moved to Hawaii because of a new job. He had actually been hearing God speak to him about moving for several years, but he had put it off. He was "kicking the can down the road," hoping the problem would go away by itself.

He knew it was time for a change.

His marriage was not doing well. He was running with the wrong friends and getting into situations that left him compromising his faith.

Finally, a job came up in Hawaii that gave him the impetus to pull the trigger and start a new life. After a few months of transition, he relocated with his family. He also got involved in a good church, got his marriage back on track, and renewed his faith.

But within six weeks, his new job dried up.

I remember sitting with him. He was moaning and groaning. "God brought me here because of this new job, and now it's gone! I really thought this was God, but now look! I'm without a job!"

"Wait a minute!" I said. "Didn't God prompt you to move to Hawaii?"

"Yes."

"And you obeyed?"

"Reluctantly, but yes."

"Maybe the new job was not the real goal. It wasn't what was most important. He wanted you to move here for a new life, a new beginning, and a better relationship with your wife. Let God open up another job for you before you make a hasty decision and miss what God planned to happen . . . along the way."

Effective or Efficient?

God's main goal is often not leisure. It's likeness. It's not living an easy life. It is living an effective one.

Do you know the difference between being *efficient* and being *effective*? The words sound similar at first. But they have very different meanings.

We can have *efficient* communication systems, computers, and satellites. We can have efficient companies, water purification systems, and nuclear programs. But although we are efficient, we are not necessarily effective. We are failing in our families, our marriages, our relationships, morals, and manners.

Here's the difference:

Being efficient is *doing things right*.
Being effective is *doing the right things*.

Once a man came running into his doctor's office. "Doctor, quick! Give me the best thing you've got for the hiccups."

"The best thing?" the doctor asked.

"Yes! The absolute best thing."

"You want it now?"

"Now!"

The doctor clenched his fist and walloped the man as hard as he could in the stomach.

The man doubled over in a coughing fit. "What did you do that for?" he wheezed.

"You wanted the best thing for hiccups, right?" the doctor said.

"Yes!"

"Well, do you have the hiccups anymore?"

"No," said the ailing man. "But my wife waiting in the car still does!"

The doctor was efficient but not very effective.

Three Points in Living Life Along the Way

I'm a multitasking person by nature. I have my smartphone linked into my computer, which automatically syncs my calendar so I can multitask everything. I have a wonderful assistant who schedules each day down to the minute. I like to get lots done.

But in spite of all that efficiency, I constantly need to gauge my *effectiveness*. The big question is "Am I spending my time not only doing things right but doing the right things?"

Here are three crucial emphases to living life along the way. Let's look at each one.

1. Focus

He who tills his land will have plenty of bread, but he who pursues worthless things lacks sense.

Proverbs 12:11

Steve Jobs, the late entrepreneurial genius behind Apple's success, was fired in 1984, but when the company's stock fell through the floor, he was rehired in 1997. The biography of his life by Walter Isaacson tells the story of that reentry. Upon seeing the multitude of peripherals Apple was engaged in, barefooted Steve Jobs walked to a white board, drew a square, and divided it into quadrants. In one square, he wrote "pro." Next to it, "consumer." In the bottom square, he penned "desktop," and in the final square, "mobile." He then turned to his engineers and said, "Make one Apple product for each box and cancel the rest."

Focus.

It worked. Although Apple added three more initiatives to the original four, in fourteen years, Apple would rise to become the world's most valuable company, worth over 500 billion dollars.

Focus. It works in every area of life. You will find this same principle peppered throughout the sacred pages as if to remind us over and over again of the importance of focus.

- "One thing . . ."
- "Set your mind . . ."
- "He set His face like a flint . . ."
- "Straightaway . . ."
- "Turn neither to the right nor to the left . . ."
- "Let your gaze be fixed in front of you . . ."
- "A double-minded man will be unstable in all his ways . . ."

157

2. Intentionality: Wherever You Are, Be There

A near second to focus is *intentionality*.

Have you ever missed something important because you were daydreaming, sleeping, or rushing to get ahead? Maybe you're sitting in church but you're checking e-mail. Or you're at home doing your devotions and you think, "I'd rather be golfing."

You're there, but not really. You skip life as it's happening and exchange the here and now for somewhere out there.

But what if there was something in the now that Jesus really wanted you to see?

This happened to me a while back. I am not really good at making my own flight arrangements. Usually my assistant, Mary, handles it all for me. But on a personal fishing trip to Alaska, I decided to be my own travel agent, and in order to show myself frugal I flew standby.

Have you ever flown standby? Usually it works out, but this time, it turned into a real circus. I made it to Seattle, and there I asked if there were any open seats to Anchorage.

"Absolutely, sir," the ticket counter attendant said with a smile. "We have seventeen seats open. Just go straight to the gate, and you'll be able to get on with no problem."

I rushed straight over to the gate and said to the person behind the counter, "I'm flying standby. I was told I could get my boarding pass here."

The gate attendant typed into her computer. "Hmmm," she said with a frown. "Doesn't look like we have any seats open. Why don't you take a seat. We'll let you know if any openings become available."

"I was just at the main ticket counter. The agent there told me there were seventeen open seats . . . seven-TEEN," I said, emphasizing the count of open seats.

"Sorry," she replied. "Everything looks tight. We are sold out, and to be honest, I don't know if you are going to get on. There's another flight in the morning that looks open."

"No, no, no," I said. "Seventeen are open." I was fuming. "You should check your computer again. The fish are waiting for me. I've really got to get on this plane."

"Take a seat, sir," she said firmly. "I'll check the computer, and if anything opens up, I'll let you know."

I sat down and waited. I paced and tapped my foot. Ten minutes passed and I returned to the counter. "Any seats available yet? Can you check your computer one more time?"

"It's the same computer," she said. "I just checked it a few minutes ago."

"But could you check just one more time?"

"I don't think so, sir."

"But there were seventeen!"

"All right," she said, I'm sure just to humor me. "I'll check again. What's your name?" She exhaled loudly.

"Wayne Cordeiro."

"No way!" Her tone suddenly changed and she looked up at me.

"Why?" I said.

"Because I just finished reading your book *The Divine Mentor*! What a great book about being like Jesus!"

I thought, *"Oh no!"*

"Do you know the best part of the book?" she said. "It was when you wrote that there are some Bible mentors who will help you with unexpected problems as you read your daily devotions. I loved it!"

She typed into her keyboard again. "But sorry—there are still no seats open for this flight."

I turned around, feeling embarrassed, and walked away to take a seat again. Before I got three steps, another woman off to my left said, "Pastor Wayne! Hey—it's Pastor Wayne!"

"Oh no, not again," I whispered.

She ran right up to me and gave me a big hug. "I'm from Kauai," she said, "and I watch you on television all the time. I just need to tell you how much your TV show has helped my life."

"I hope it will help mine," I said meekly.

Life happens in between the fishing and getting on the plane. If we are not careful to understand that, we can miss some of God's biggest plans. My goal was to get to the fish. I wanted to do it as quickly and efficiently as possible. But God was inviting me to exchange my desire to be efficient with my understanding of *effective* ministry—in this case, never forgetting who I was or who I represent. Maybe it was to slow me down. Maybe it was to encourage some people who worked tirelessly behind a ticket counter appeasing irate customers all day.

Ouch.

3. Lordship: Jesus Alone

Ever come across Scripture verses that baffle you? Well, here's a doozy.

> No one can say, "Jesus is Lord," except by the Holy Spirit.
>
> 1 Corinthians 12:3

I never understood what it meant. Surely anyone can say "Jesus is Lord," and it doesn't require the Holy Spirit's assistance!

But now I would find out.

When Anna and I were first married she worked at a locksmith shop. One of the benefits was that she'd bring home samples of locks and I would install them on our doors, windows, screens, walls, ceilings . . .

One evening, we were running late for a dinner engagement. (Not my fault.) I was downstairs pacing the living room, attempting to adjust my rhythm to that of my new bride. The longer I waited, the more she delayed, and the more she delayed, the higher my blood pressure soared.

Finally, Anna sprinted down the stairs, we ran out the front door, locked it behind us, and jumped in our car.

"All right," I said. "Give me the keys."

"Keys?" she said. "You're supposed to have the keys."

"I don't have the keys. You're the wife—you always have the keys."

She looked in her purse. "I don't have the keys."

I growled.

We made a call from the neighbor's (this was before the advent of the cell phone), and soon the locksmith arrived. Sixty dollars later, Anna and I retrieved the wayward keys and started out again for dinner. (Now we were REALLY late.) We didn't converse much that evening. It was a bit chilly.

Several months later we went to visit my brother in the San Francisco Bay area. By the time we got into the city, the freeways had come to a standstill. I was about to experience the Super Bowl of gridlocks. We were baking in the sweltering afternoon sun on the interstate, the white lines melting into the asphalt beneath.

After what seemed like hours, the traffic began to move. I saw an exit coming up and said, "Do you think that's our exit?"

Besides not arriving during rush hour, there's one more thing you don't want to do around a big city. You don't want to take the wrong exit. Commit that error and you'll have to drive to Tijuana in order to get back on . . . and I don't speak Spanish.

"Is this the one we take?"

"I think so," she said.

"Check the map quick! We're almost there."

Glancing down, she said, "I think this is it."

I yanked on the wheel, but within minutes, I felt that something was not right. We wove our way through a run-down neighborhood filled with graffiti. Fuming at my navigator's sheer inability with maps, I pulled the car over at a gas station, slammed on the brakes, and sighed, "God, it's this woman you gave me!"

Jesus spoke to my heart and asked, "Wayne, who is your lord?"

> We give lordship away far too freely.

"You are!" I rumbled.

Jesus spoke quietly: "Your lord is the one who *controls your disposition, your decision making, and your choices.* Have you noticed that your relationship with your wife went from good to bad in just one exit? Whoever has that much power over you is the one you have bowed to as your 'lord.'"

Then Jesus took me back to the time when the keys were locked inside the house. He said, "Who was your lord then? Who did you give control to for your whole evening? Who controlled your relationship with your wife?"

I got it.

The lost keys had become my lord that night. And the missed exit . . . I allowed both to usurp lordship away from Jesus. We will have many lost keys and wrong exits in our lives, but there can be only one Lord.

We give lordship away far too freely.

See if you can recognize these lords:

- A friend's bad attitude that ruins ours.
- Another Christian who acts horribly causes us to stay away from church.

- A driver who cut us off on the freeway turns us into an angry avenger as we tailgate him for a few miles just to let him know our displeasure.
- A boss's decision that we disagree with gives us the rationale to gossip and complain.

Who's your lord?

Remember the lyrics written by Linda Lee Johnson a few years ago?

He is Lord, He is Lord![1]

Maybe it's time we sing it again, and this time, by the power of the Holy Spirit. Ask Jesus to be Lord again. Ask Him to help you with lost keys and wrong exits. You won't always see the reason for things that happen, but if you can see His hand, it won't matter.

Lead Me to the Rock

A dad was landscaping his backyard and wanted to teach his ten-year-old son how to develop a strong work ethic. Buried in the middle of their backyard was a big rock. "Son," he said. "I want you to do everything you can to move that rock to the side of the house."

The son pushed the rock. He dug around it and tried to lift it out. He got a crowbar and tried to pry it out. Finally he said, "Dad, I've tried everything. I can't move it."

"No," the dad said. "You haven't tried everything. Try again to move that rock."

1. "He Is Lord," Claire Cloninger, Linda Lee Johnson, and Tom Fettke, ©1986 Word Music LLC.

Again the son tried. He pushed, and dug again, and pried again. With sweat on his brow, he came back to his dad. He said, "Dad, I tried everything and I still can't move it."

"You still haven't tried everything," the father said.

"No, I tried everything," said the son.

"Try again," said the father.

Ask Jesus to help you to see Him along the way.

The son went back to the rock and kicked it, punched it, and yelled at it. He got a hammer out of the garage and tried to break the rock. Exhausted, the son came back to his father. "Dad, now I've tried everything. There's no way I can move it."

"You still haven't tried everything," the father said.

"Dad—I've tried everything!"

"No, there's still one more thing you haven't tried."

"What haven't I tried?"

The father smiled.

"You haven't asked me for help."

Ask Jesus to help you to see Him along the way. Ask the Holy Spirit to give you the power to make Jesus Lord, not only in church, but when there are wrong exits, lost keys, and others' failures.

Ask Him.

Questions for individual reflection or group discussion:

1. John Lennon of the Beatles was a controversial figure, but one of his quotes was "Life is what happens while you're busy making other plans." What do you think he meant by that?

2. Have you ever been on your way to do something, only to find that something else more important happened along the way? Can you share the story of that?

3. What's the difference between being *efficient* and being *effective*? Where do you think we need to be more effective?

4. What's important about always being completely "there"?

5. What's the difference between being busy and being hurried?

6. How can you remember to keep Jesus as Lord when everything else seems to vie for control?

CHAPTER 11

THE WAY HOME

> Create in me a clean heart, O God, and renew a steadfast spirit within me. Do not cast me away from Your presence and do not take Your Holy Spirit from me. Restore to me the joy of Your salvation and sustain me with a willing spirit.
>
> Psalm 51:10–12

Let me preach to the choir for a few minutes. (Sometimes the choir needs it more than the congregation.)

One anonymous quote on leadership has incessantly reminded me of the basics: *"The most conspicuous way to know when a person is ready to lead others is when he is able to lead himself."*

I like that.

It's the log-in-the-eye syndrome of Matthew 7. Jesus said we should take the telephone pole out of our own eye before performing surgery to remove the lint in our neighbor's eye.

But it's our human tendency to start off thinking that way. We often want to hold a clinic to instruct others about cleanliness when our house looks like the remains after Hurricane Andrew.

We counsel others on their ineptitudes while we are oblivious to the same in ourselves.

We often talk about leading others to Christ. Here's the key: Can you lead yourself to Christ?

Oh, I'm not talking about a first-time acceptance of Christ. I'm referring to re-engaging when you've gotten detached. It's about renewing. It's about finding yourself in a drift. Can you lead yourself back home? When you realize you've been in a funk, can you lift yourself up and find your way back? It's about correcting back. It's about pressing in and concentrating your efforts until you've gained Christ's presence again. That's the renewal that must become a common experience—as common as drifting. It cannot be foreign. Renewal has to be as frequent as the morning sunrise, not like a solar eclipse.

God designed us for renewal.

Stanford Medical Center recently reported that our outer layer of skin renews itself every seven days, and every cell in our body is completely renewed every seven years. God continued on that theme of renewals in groupings of sevens. Every seven days, we are to cease and desist. He called that a Sabbath. In the Old Testament, every seven years all debts were to be forgiven. (How I wish all banks were Jewish!) All that to say: Renewal and new beginnings are to be far more frequent than we'd imagine.

God loves renewal. Like the Prodigal Son in Luke 15, we experience joy and renewal when we lead ourselves back home.

The story is told of a cowboy who was to bake the morning's biscuits for the rest of the wranglers who were working hard on the range. When they came in for breakfast, the biscuits looked like wafers, flat as crackers. He had inadvertently left out a few crucial ingredients.

"What happened to these biscuits?!" demanded one of the cowpunchers. "They're as hard as hockey pucks."

"I'm not sure," said the amateur baker. "They were in the oven, and they squatted to rise, but I guess they just got cooked in the squat!"

We can get stuck in the squat too. Without leading ourselves back to Christ consistently, our inside slump becomes caramelized. Our frustration can form a glaze on the interior without it showing much on the exterior. We trade content for image and we rationalize the hockey pucks rather than redoing the batch of biscuits. It's easier and requires less of us.

We've become better at making excuses than making changes.

Knockoffs are difficult to spot and are always cheaper to attain, and cosmetic Christianity is adequate fare for many of today's believers.

But in the end, Christians will not be counted. *They will be weighed.* God looks not at the outward appearance. He weighs our motives. He searches the heart.

That kind of heart won't be found at the cosmetic counter. It's only found when we return home.

Let me pose a few questions to help us apply this to our lives:

- When I find myself consumed by the world, can I lead myself back to Christ?
- When I am bitter or offended and find myself still religious but far from God, can I lead myself back?
- When I am caught in a spirit of anger or righteous in my rancor, can I lead myself back to Jesus?
- When I feel separated from my spouse, and I know it is not right but I am still angry, can I lead myself back to Christ and back to a healthy relationship?

All of us like sheep have gone astray, each of us has turned to his own way; but the Lord has caused the iniquity of us all to fall on Him.

Isaiah 53:6

169

The Lord likens us to sheep.

I've always wondered why He juxtaposes us with those woolly creatures that dot the Judean hillsides. Likening us to sheep isn't the most flattering comparison. I've always thought German shepherds would suit us better. But sheep? Sheep are frail. Vulnerable. They're accident prone and easily lost. I don't know much about sheep, but one thing I do know . . .

Sheep need a shepherd.

That's the reason Jesus calls us His sheep. On our own, we drift like a kite without a string or a leaf in a storm. Robert Robinson described us well in 1758, when he penned these stanzas of "Come, Thou Fount of Every Blessing":

> Prone to wander, Lord, I feel it,
> Prone to leave the God I love.
> Here's my heart, oh, take and seal it,
> Seal it for Thy courts above.

Causes of Drift

Why do we drift? Let me suggest three common causes.

1. Unguarded Strengths

Careless stewardship of our strengths can become our greatest weakness. A person with the gift of mercy, unguarded, can begin to feel guilty for all the things they are not able to do. They will feel overwhelmed by their inability to alleviate the suffering of others.

The gift of wisdom, unguarded, will turn to pride. We see that in Solomon's life. What began as deep insight ended in tragedy. His taken-for-granted wisdom eroded in the end into idolatry and leniency.

A gift of influence, unprotected, morphs eventually into the need to control. The strength of leadership unmaintained can spiral into unaccountability. Even compassion can devolve into sin.

I first began pastoral ministry at thirty-one years of age. I was working late one night at the office, finishing a message, when I heard a knock on the side door. Wondering who would be visiting at that hour, I cautiously opened the door to find a young woman from our church crying.

"Come in," I said, ushering her out of the dark.

She was a beautiful young lady, whose kindness and hospitality toward others I had often noticed in our fledgling congregation.

"Tell me what's causing you so much sorrow," I said to her.

She began relating to me the abuse her husband had been piling on her and the anger that forced her to distance herself from him. As she continued, I could feel myself not only getting angry at this unfeeling husband, but I could sense a deep compassion for this dear woman who could no longer sustain the mistreatment. I felt a deep love for her welling up inside me, and I wanted to somehow right this terrible wrong. She needed a protector, a strong anchor in her storm-tossed heart.

Sin usually starts with innocence.

Just then, I sensed the presence of His wisdom, and heard Jesus say, "Don't love her with your love. *Love her only with Mine.* Your love is corruptible. *Mine is not.*"

I quickly made the correction, and we solved the problem in a way that may have saved my marriage. I knew at that moment if I didn't get back home to Jesus, I would have crossed a line that could have become the end of my ministry. Once the Holy Spirit is ignored and the line is crossed, it becomes increasingly difficult to find your way back.

Sin seldom starts out with evil. . . . *Sin usually starts with innocence.*

An affair often begins with an innocent conversation that progresses to an innocent meal together. Then to more time talking, then laughter, text messages, and more time together. Somewhere along the way, you cross a Rubicon, a line of no return.

Drift can begin with

- unguarded friendships
- unguarded strengths
- unguarded compassion
- unguarded hearts

Now leading yourself back to Christ becomes the most important thing you can ever do for your future.

2. Stolen Joy

Restore to me the joy of your salvation and sustain me with a willing spirit.

Psalm 51:12

Sometimes drift is caused by the enemy embezzling our joy. The devil cannot steal our salvation—it's wrapped up tight in the sacrifice of Christ. So he approaches from another angle. He steals the joy of our salvation, and we give up on it ourselves.

- The adversary has no authority to steal our marriage, so he steals the joy from our marriage, and we surrender it ourselves.
- He has no power to steal our ministry, so he pilfers the joy of our ministry, and we drop out ourselves.

Guard the joy of walking with Jesus. It will be stalked and sometimes beleaguered and battered, but guard your joy.

Joy is distinctly different from happiness.

Happiness comes from happenstances. It rises from happenings. It also falls with the same. But joy comes from the Spirit of God. Nehemiah 8:10 reminds us that the "joy of the Lord is our strength." It is the joy of the Lord that the Spirit can convert into life-sustaining power.

Joy is sourced in Jesus, not in circumstances.

You'll sense it. When the thief is near, stay close to home.

The thief comes to only steal and kill and destroy; I came that they may have life, and have it abundantly.

John 10:10

3. Not Recognizing His Voice

The sheep follow Him because they know His voice.

John 10:4

In Margaret Feinberg's book, *Scouting the Divine*, she tells of an encounter with a shepherdess near Portland, Oregon. On a tour of the sheep ranch, the shepherdess and Margaret climbed muddy hills to a knoll from which they could see sheep atop the nearby hills.

The shepherdess whispered, "As soon as they hear my voice, they'll come running."

Margaret wondered if the sheep would confirm the words of Jesus when He said that sheep know their shepherd's voice. Sure enough, when the shepherdess called, "Sheep, sheep, sheep," the sheep ran toward her.[1]

Can you recognize the voice of the Shepherd? He's ever-present and always accessible. The question is never "God, are You speaking?" The real question is "Am I listening?"

1. Margaret Feinberg, *Scouting the Divine* (Grand Rapids, MI: Zondervan, 2009), 26–27.

He will counsel you, comfort you, warn you. In the midst of an imperceptible drift toward a potentially dangerous relationship, can you hear His voice? Can you recognize the sound of His call? When you do, you have direction.

Then follow, and at times . . .

Run.

Three Truths About Lost and Found

> Act, and God will act.
>
> Joan of Arc

I've discovered a few things about getting lost . . . and about getting found again. The Shepherd is faithful to search, but getting found will require some cooperation on our part. Always remember: Although growth may be automatic, *maturity is optional.* Faith is linked to action, not inaction. Waiting on God cannot be confused with complacency, and procrastination is not a synonym of patience.

So with that in mind, let's take a look at the following truths:

1. If Drifting Is a Pattern, Intentional Correction Is Needed

- Are you still struggling this year with a problem you had last year?
- Do you have the same anger that destroys relationships as you had five years ago?
- Are you struggling with the same grumbling attitude as always?
- Are you still in the habit of expressing anger for what you feel are personal infractions against you?

Then it is less a problem and more a spirit. No, it may not always be an evil or demonic one, but it is still a *spirit*. A spirit doesn't necessarily need to possess you, but it can *oppress* you!

- A habit of anger left unresolved can bring a contentious spirit.
- A pattern of lasciviousness or viewing pornography can summon a spirit of lust.
- A routine of internalizing irritations beckons a spirit of bitterness.

Never forget: It is not sin that destroys God's people. *It is unresolved sin that does.*

So we need God's intervention and His divine correction. The process of being corrected will not be enjoyable, *but it is eternally beneficial.*

> No discipline seems pleasant at the time, but painful. Later on, however, it produces a harvest of righteousness and peace for those who have been trained by it.
>
> Hebrews 12:11 NIV

In the Bedouin sheepherders' culture, they know that if the sheep are flocked around the shepherd, predators will not attack, because the shepherd is there. But predators will be patient and wait for a lamb to stray.

It is not sin that destroys God's people. It is unresolved sin that does.

The shepherd will leave the ninety and nine in the open field and go after that one lamb and bring it back. He will forgive it, love it, and say, "Stay! Because I know that if you stray again it may be the end of your life."

Now, if this lamb has a propensity to stray, and if the shepherd finds it straying one time . . . two times . . . ten times . . . then he knows that the future of this lamb is in grave jeopardy. A calculating predator hidden among the crags surely is plotting his next move while preparing the mint jelly. The lamb will soon be lunch.

> If you are in a season of correction or brokenness, press in to the Shepherd.

When the shepherd realizes the fatal pattern, he will hold the lamb firmly and break its front leg. A struggle ensues, but the shepherd will methodically splint the broken leg, wrap it, and return to the flock carrying the wayward lamb on his shoulders. He continues to cradle the lame returnee in his arms until the healing is complete. And when the prodigal is finally able to sustain its own weight once again, a transformation has taken place along the way. A new propensity has replaced the old pattern.

The lamb stays intimately close to the shepherd.

And all that has taken place was because of love. At the moment of its injury, I'm certain the lamb came to other conclusions, but later on, the lamb comprehends.

Faith is living in advance what we will only understand in reverse.

> What shall we say then? Are we to continue in sin so that grace may increase? May it never be!
>
> Romans 6:1–2

God loves us just as we are, but He loves us too much to let us stay the same. God's *correction* is synonymous with His *protection*.

It's easy to slip into a cheap grace where we define God as a lenient power whose sole responsibility is to give us immunity from negative consequences. We slowly, over the years, create God *in our image*. But get used to God's correction. It's not a foreign affair, but a regular one.

I remember taking that golf lesson before moving to Hawaii. The instructor had to correct me dozens and dozens of times, and often for the same error! But as soon as I would say, "Stop correcting me!" . . . the lesson would be over.

If you are in a season of correction or brokenness, press in to the Shepherd. Even if you are lame, draw close. Learn from Him and catch His ways. The sooner the better.

The second thing I've discovered about getting lost . . . and about getting found, is this:

2. The Road I Am on Determines My Destination

But now what are you doing on the road to Egypt, to drink the waters of the Nile? Or what are you doing on the road to Assyria, to drink the waters of the Euphrates?

Jeremiah 2:18–19

Here's how to find your road: At the end of your life, when family and friends gather to memorialize you, what do you want to be known for? What do you wish people to remember you by that would separate you from the rest?

- Running marathons?
- Making more and more money?
- Having hundreds of Facebook friends?
- Traveling the world?
- Successfully running your own business?

These may be beneficial in varying aspects, so it's not an either/or. But wouldn't you rather be remembered for being these:

- A great parent who influenced your children deeply toward the faith
- An authentic follower of Jesus Christ who lived without pretense

- A spouse who remained committed throughout your life
- A wise person

If these are some of the characteristics you desire, then be sure that you're not on the road to Egypt! Do you have plans in place, goals, or friendships developed to help you get there? If not, be certain that you check the highway signs to ensure that you're not on a motorway to Assyria.

Here are a few misguided roadways:

Let's say a single woman says, "I want to meet and one day marry a great Christian guy who really has his act together." That is her intention. But then she dates any old boy who asks her out—just as long as he's good-looking.

Egypt is right down the road a spell.

Or let's say a husband announces, "I want my kids to respect me when they grow up," but then he flirts with other women, slips into pornography, and frequently loses his temper.

Assyria is just around the bend.

A woman says, "I really want to have a great relationship with my husband." But then she makes the children a priority over him and their friendship diminishes to the point where they do little more than coexist.

Or perhaps a young Christian says, "I really want to develop a deep and lasting intimacy with God." But then he gets up late every morning, checks last night's sports scores, scans the news, and rushes into the day while checking his Facebook page every fifteen minutes.

Newlyweds may be determined to be financially secure by the time they reach their parents' age. But then they buy everything they see, falling into a lifestyle of credit card abuse and debt.

I hope they packed enough for the sandstorms of Egypt and the deserts of Assyria.

3. We Seldom Get Lost Intentionally

Sheep have a tendency to drift—but not intentionally, mind you. It is like a constant current that we need to resist with unrelenting vigilance.

Recently I noticed that my devotions, although still regular, were not as deep and fresh as they once were. It didn't seem like I was absorbing anything from the Word of God. No nuggets of wisdom were finding their way through my brain and into my soul. My devotions seemed like religious activity, but that was all.

My love for Christ was still there, but my joy of sitting at His feet on a daily basis had dulled.

So I knew I was drifting. Oh, it's undetectable at first. Sometimes you feel it, but it's usually later rather than sooner. Although a drift moves at a snail's pace, it does have a pace to it, and ignored, it will cross the Rubicon sooner than you expect.

My goal is to mark up a Bible every five years. As I do my devotions, I write on the pages my thoughts, feelings, questions, answers, insights, and problems—everything—to the point where my writing fills the margins of the pages. Then it is time to get another Bible.

So I bit the bullet and went out and bought a new Bible and a journal. Clean pages, no markings, no notes from previous devotional findings. The white spaces around the verses were crying for new revelation and new inspiration. That challenge was enough for me to renew my zest for the Word and get going again.

The Meeting Place

Several years ago our family went to Disneyland. We were at an area in the park near a Texaco gas station. It was 10 AM. We were just beginning our day, and I said to our kids, "Hey, listen! Everybody is going to split up, and we will probably get separated from one another. But at 3 PM we will all meet right here under the Texaco star. Everybody got it? Just like the magi in the Christmas story. Meet right underneath the star."

If you get lost—and I'm not talking about at Disneyland—do you know where to meet back up again?

I remember one of the best commitments I made with my wife early on (while she was still my fiancée). I said, "We are like sheep, and one day we may get separated from each other. If that ever happens, *promise that we will meet again at Calvary. And if I get there before you, I will wait for you. If you get there before me, please wait for me.*"

We both understood what that meant.

Calvary is the place where barriers are removed. It's where God and man connect again deeply. At the cross, redemption took place, but not only once. It can take place again and again. Calvary is a place where the issue is not "Who's right?" but "What's right?" There, it isn't about us. It's about Jesus.

Know well the road back to Calvary. Make it a commitment between you and your spouse, between you and your children, between you and your leaders.

- Are you drifting in your marriage? *Meet back at Calvary.*
- Are you discouraged in a relationship that is consuming you from the inside out? Find yourself again *at Calvary.*
- Are you uncomfortable about the future? Lead yourself *back to Calvary* and find comfort there.

A Most Expensive Painting

A wealthy widower had a son whom he loved deeply. Among other things, the father was an art aficionado, so he traveled the world collecting priceless paintings by Rembrandt, Monet, and Van Gogh. Back home, he decorated his vast estate with the treasured art.

Years passed and the son grew up. The nation was now torn by war, and the son enlisted to defend his country. After a few months of combat, the father received a telegram reporting, sadly, that his son had been killed in action.

Deep discouragement and mourning set in. The house that was once filled with the laughter of his young boy was now silent and hollow.

Several winters passed and the father was facing another Christmas alone when a knock came at the door. A young soldier stood on the front step.

"Sir," the young man said, "I am so sorry to bother you." He was carrying something tucked under his arm. "I was in the same platoon as your son. He and I became very close friends, and he often told me about your love for art. I am not that good of an artist, but one evening during a lull in the action, I sketched a portrait of your son. It's not much, but I thought you would like to have it."

The father thanked him and the soldier left. Inside the estate, he unwrapped the gift. The sketch remarkably resembled his son in every way. Tears came to the father's eyes. It became his most precious art piece. He hung it over the mantel of his fireplace. Every day he looked at it, and it brought him much consolation and joy.

Some years later, the father passed away. Art collectors from all over the country flew in to buy the quality art that was to be auctioned. Prospective buyers filled the room waiting to place a bid for a Rembrandt or Monet. To everyone's surprise, the auction began not with what they had expected, but with a piece of art that wasn't on the list—the sketch done by the young soldier.

The art collectors looked at each other bewildered. You could hear them, annoyed and impatient, saying, "We didn't travel this far to purchase an amateur's sketch. Let's get on with the auction!"

The auctioneer pressed on. "We will start this bidding at one hundred dollars," he said.

No one bid. There was silence. "Let's get on with it!" someone cried out.

Again the auctioneer said, "One hundred dollars is the starting bid."

Slowly, an old man from the back raised his hand and said, "I have been the neighbor of this family for years. I knew the father. I knew the son. I knew the mother before she passed away. They were dear, dear people. I will buy that sketch. I don't have much money, but I will pay the one hundred dollars. I would very much like to have it."

"The bid is one hundred," said the auctioneer. "Am I bid one hundred and fifty? Anyone?"

No one said anything. "Let him have it so we can move on!" the other collectors said, looking at their watches and tapping their feet.

"Going once! Going twice!" The auctioneer hit the gavel, but instead of saying "Gone!" to everyone's surprise, he said, "The auction is now over!"

The crowd started to protest. "Wait a minute," said a collector. "It hasn't even begun! Let's get on with the good stuff!"

"Sorry," said the auctioneer. "The auction is over."

"It can't be," complained another collector. "What's going on?"

"It's very simple," said the auctioneer. "According to the father's written will—'When you auction all my paintings, start with the sketch of my son. . . . *The one who takes the son gets it all.*'"

In the end, it all comes back to Jesus, pure and simple.

Questions for individual reflection or group discussion:

1. Why is it so easy to drift?

2. The drift never starts out intentionally. What are the ways we can catch ourselves before it has gone too far?

3. How can God's correction be uncomfortable—even painful—yet also beneficial?

4. Discuss the difference between punishment and discipline.

5. What does it mean to meet back at Calvary?

CHAPTER 12

JESUS NEVER CHANGES

He made known His ways to Moses,
His acts to the sons of Israel.

Psalm 103:7

A friend from my church and I were in Japan, walking and talking in an over-crowded subway hallway. This was his first time in this beautiful country, and his first time in the Shinjuku train station, where over three million people pass through every day.

As we walked, my friend kept running into people. I soon realized the reason for the collisions, although he was oblivious to the dilemma and kept dodging the oncoming traffic. Finally, I said, "Derrek, do you know what country you are in?"

"Why sure," he said. "Japan!"

I continued, "This is not America. What side of the sidewalk do people usually walk on?"

"The right."

I said. "In this country, they walk on the left. Are you starting to see the bigger picture here?"

It was like going the wrong way down a one-way street! As soon as he switched sides and walked on the left, everything cleared up. No more dodging. No more bumping.

The kingdom of God is like that. It's a different culture altogether than that of the world, and in order to navigate your life as a Christ-follower, you need to make some changes. You will need to realize the country you are in and walk accordingly. Learning that will make the difference between cooperating with your surroundings and colliding with them.

Unlearning and Relearning

Alvin Toffler, who wrote the groundbreaking book *Future Shock,* said, "The illiterate of the twenty-first century will not be those who cannot read and write, but those who cannot *learn, unlearn, and relearn.*"

Some of the things that worked for you in the past will work against you in the future, and some activities that were helpful in the past will now be harmful to you.

In my youth, I moved from Hawaii to Oregon, where I attended high school. The athletes all seemed taller, sleeker, and faster. I had to train longer, stay later, and work harder than any of the other athletes just to stay even. I became a fierce competitor.

But later I entered the ministry, and what used to work for me was now working against me. Working longer and harder used to bring me trophies, but now only brought suspicion, criticism, and broken relationships. I had to unlearn some things and relearn.

When I was younger, I could get away with eating whatever I wanted and still remain thin and physically nimble. Now I just look at a hamburger on the menu and I gain ten pounds.

- My diet that included large fries and a milkshake used to do nothing. Now it does everything.
- I used to break my leg in the morning and I'd be playing soccer by the afternoon. But now I heal in a matter of a few years.
- I used to stay up until midnight on December 31 to welcome in the New Year. Now I let it welcome itself.

Likewise, walking with Jesus requires massive life changes from the way I used to live. And that requires choices. Not casual ones. Real ones! When you choose to walk with Christ, when you want more than the illusion of being close to Him, when you want to walk near to Him in reality, you will need to pull the trigger.

> **Walking with Jesus requires massive life changes from the way I used to live.**

It's not about reading the Bible more, praying more, having more faith, or doing more, more, more. It's about getting back to Jesus and surrendering to Him completely.

Don't do it halfway. Think about it . . .

- When God decided to make man in His image, He didn't do it halfway.
- When God chose to redeem mankind, He didn't do it halfway.
- When Jesus suffered for your sins and mine, He didn't do it halfway.
- When Jesus testifies on our behalf on that day when we stand before the Judge of the universe, we don't want Him to do it halfway!

Isn't it time we choose to be all for Jesus? Isn't it time we dedicate our lives to the One who dedicated His to us?

Now Is the Time

There's an old hymn that I love. "I'll Wish I Had Given Him More" was written in 1948 by Grace Reese Adkins. Its lyrics remind us of that day when we will look back over our lives, and we will do it with joy or regret. The choice is ours, but we must make that choice today, not tomorrow. The hymn's lyrics never cease to stir my heart.

I received Christ when I was nineteen, and the only regret I have is that I didn't receive Him sooner. Solomon writes wisely, in Ecclesiastes 12, these profound yet almost humorous words:

> Remember also your Creator in the days of your youth, before the evil days come and the years draw near when you will say, "I have no delight in them."

Now, you have to read these next words slowly to catch what Solomon is talking about. He encourages us to serve our Creator before we are old:

- "In the day that the watchmen of the house tremble." Here he is describing old men who tremble when they walk.
- "And mighty men stoop." Or when our backs are curved and we walk bent over.
- "The grinding ones stand idle because they are few." Here he describes the loss of teeth as the years go by. (Remember, they had few dentists and no dentures.)
- "And those who look through windows grow dim." These are the eyes of the elderly that grow dim with cataracts or other diseases of advanced age.
- "The doors on the street are shut as the sound of the grinding mill is low," speaks of hearing loss.

- "And one will arise at the sound of the bird, and all the daughters of song will sing softly." Older people rise early and their sense of hearing diminishes.
- "And the caperberry is ineffective." The caperberry was used as an aphrodisiac.

In other words, don't wait until you are old before you decide to give it all to the Lord. Start serving Him long before you lose your health or have little energy. Give Him everything in the prime of your life, not at the lowest point; give Him your zenith, not leftovers. If you're still considering giving it all to Jesus when the caperberries lose their effectiveness, you're way too slow.

> **Give Him everything in the prime of your life.**

Staying Steady in a World of Change

In 1964, Bob Dylan released a song called "The Times They Are a-Changin'." He could have written the same song today. Times really are a-changin'. Some changes are harmless, and we just need to adapt and adjust. But some things must never change.

It's good to know Jesus never changes. And that's the thought I want to end with as I close this book. As you journey toward a pure and simple devotion to Christ, it's good to know that Jesus never changes. His love is always pure. His goodness never falters. His excellence is unsurpassed. He is the same yesterday, today, and forever. And though times change, Jesus stays the same.

> I, the Lord, do not change.
>
> Malachi 3:6

Jesus is beautifully predictable.

- I know that when I stray I can run to Him with all my fractured thinking, and He will always receive me with open arms.
- If I am hurting, He will comfort me, bring healing, and urge me onward.
- If I make excuses, He will not give in. I must change. Not Him.

Jesus is beautifully predictable. The Bible calls Him our trustworthy, dependable, unchangeable, immutable God.

That's Jesus, pure and simple.

Getting Ready

We are in the last chapter—not only in this book, but in the shelf life of mankind. I can't accurately detect exactly where in that last chapter we are, but we are in the last chapter.

Here is what Timothy says about these last days:

> But realize this, that in the last days difficult times will come. For men will be lovers of self, lovers of money, boastful, arrogant, revilers, disobedient to parents, ungrateful, unholy, unloving, irreconcilable, malicious gossips, without self-control, brutal, haters of good, treacherous, reckless, conceited, lovers of pleasure rather than lovers of God, holding to a form of godliness, although they have denied its power.
>
> 2 Timothy 3:1–5

Note Timothy's description. Things go from bad to worse. We see this happening even now. Morality has decreased and worldliness has increased. The line between right and wrong has been blurred.

Families have started to decline. Faith is diminished in its priority, and pleasing Jesus declines in preeminence, and now we have collisions.

In order to clear things up, God allows things to be shaken up.

> When God spoke from Mount Sinai His voice shook the earth, but now He makes another promise: "Once again I will shake not only the earth but the heavens also." This means that all of creation will be shaken and removed, so that only unshakable things will remain.
>
> Hebrews 12:26–27 NLT

God may use a failing economy, the unraveling of the fabric of our society, or a meltdown in our leadership. We have seen it in the history of the church as well. About every 500 years, God has a rummage sale with the church. There's a shake-up, a culling of the useless and unusable, and then there's room for a fresh move of God.

- In AD 550, Pope Gregory cleaned out the political maneuverings in the Catholic Church.
- There was the Great Schism in AD 1054.
- Followed by the Reformation of the 1500s.
- And we are due for another shake-up.

Why? Because in these last days there will be an increasing sense of *spiritual neutrality*. Christians become ambivalent on what is moral and immoral, right and wrong, wise or unwise. Human motives and political tactics trump holiness in our denominations and churches and no one notices.

But John the revelator warns us of the lukewarm stance that will be taken by many churches and Christians that he labels the *apostasy* of the latter days. That word means "a falling away from." From what?

191

The ancient paths.

> Thus says the Lord, "Stand by the ways and see and ask for the ancient paths, where the good way is, and walk in it; and you will find rest for your souls."
>
> Jeremiah 6:16–17

That ambivalence also happened long ago. Rewind the tape for a moment to 1 Kings 18. The nation of Israel had blended into the secular society to the extent that the worshipers of God could not be distinguished from the worshipers of Baal. Israel had lost her identity.

The prophet Elijah asked,

> How long will you waver between two opinions? If the Lord is God, follow him; but if Baal is God, follow him.
>
> 1 Kings 18:21 NIV

There was to be no middle ground.

Friend, may I encourage you to realize that this is your run. You will not have another. This is your only life, and once it is done, there's *no going back*. No mulligans. No refunds. No returns.

Three Choices

So as we come to a close, please consider three choices we need to make. If we don't make these choices now, we will get caught in the vortex of the world, and once you're in, it's almost impossible to get out.

1. Choose This Day Whom You Will Serve

On May 9, 1940, at the beginning of World War II, Holland went on Radio Free Europe to declare her neutrality. The country didn't want to take sides.

The very next day, May 10, 1940, Nazi Germany launched an attack on Holland with thousands of Panzer tanks and an air strike of great force. In five days Holland fell under Nazi occupation.

When evil is present and hungry, declaring neutrality will not work. Know this: The devil will no more respect your neutrality than Hitler did Holland's. There is no middle ground. We must be pillars and supporters of truth.

2. Choose the Posture You Will Take

Your *posture* here means the attitude or disposition that you have as a believer. In the last days, how do you take a stand for truth? Will you do it with a condescending attitude? Will you be self-righteous? Will you follow Jesus with the posture of an enforcer? Will you adopt the spiritual disposition of a policeman?

It's the second most important decision you will ever make.

Your first and most important decision that you will make in life will be your decision to follow Jesus Christ. But the second most important decision will be the *attitude or disposition with which you will serve Jesus Christ.*

The first decision will affect your salvation and eternity.

The second will affect your influence and ministry.

- So be steadfast without being belligerent.
- Be teachable without being gullible.
- Be courageous without being arrogant.
- Be righteous without being self-righteous.

Work hard at keeping the Good News good news!

A seasoned preacher once said to me, "Wayne, preach nothing *up* but Jesus and nothing *down* but the devil."

I like that.

The closer you walk with Jesus, the more you will love Him, and the more you love Him, the more you will become like Him. There is a *creative affinity* in love. In other words, whatever you love the most, you become like.

For example, if you love surfing, you'll read surfing magazines. You'll buy your clothes from surf shops, you'll invest in several surfboards (after all, there will be different conditions prevailing and you need the right board). You'll look like a surfer and you'll smell like seaweed.

If you love dogs, you'll read dog magazines, own at least one, play with them, and walk them. You'll fellowship with dog lovers, attend dog conferences, travel to dog shows, and as time goes by, you may even start to look more and more like your beloved pooch.

Although I write that in humor, love does have a powerful creative affinity to it. I remember visiting with a man and his wife who had been married more than sixty-two years. Whenever they went to a restaurant, they intuitively knew what the other would order. They even finished each other's sentences. And most interesting, they looked alike!

Love's creative affinity.

That is why when a young impetuous lawyer asked Jesus if He could boil down the whole Bible into one or two commandments, Jesus answered,

> "You shall love the Lord your God with all your heart, with all your soul, and with all your mind." This is the great and foremost commandment. The second is like it, "You shall love your neighbor as yourself." On these two commandments depend the whole Law and the Prophets.
>
> Matthew 22:37–40

The more you fall in love with Jesus, the more you become like Him. It's that simple. It's pure. Fall in love more and more with Jesus. That is the simplest and most compelling way to grow.

We think that if we could only sequester ourselves in a cave and study theology all day like the monks of old, then we'd really have arrived. That may or may not help, but it is not the exhaustive answer.

I remember feeling that if I really wanted to serve God, I had to go back to seminary and get as many degrees as possible. But then I realized my motives were skewed. In my insecurity, I really didn't want to learn as much as I wanted people to call me *learn-ed*.

> **The more you fall in love with Jesus, the more you become like Him.**

Catch the difference?

One is yearning to recognize Jesus. The other is yearning for others to recognize us. One is knowing Jesus, and the other is impressing others about how much of Jesus we know.

It's like cats.

Ever notice how that furry creature rubs on your leg and does a figure eight around your ankles while you adoringly muse, "See how much that cat loves me"?

Reality check! That cat doesn't really love you. *It is simply loving itself off of you!* And in the same way, loving Jesus is not using Him to feel good about yourself. It's easy to serve at church in order to feel holy and good about ourselves. Oh, feeling good may be a result, but it cannot be our reason.

Paul reminds us in this poignant verse:

For Christ's love compels us.

2 Corinthians 5:14 NIV

There is no other reason.
It has to be Jesus, pure and simple.

3. How Will You Respond When Tested?

The truest assessment of a servant is how he responds when he is treated like one. That's the litmus test. We all want to be known as servants just so long as no one treats us like one!

But there will be tests. Not *if*, but *when*.

> But realize this, that in the last days difficult times will come.
>
> 2 Timothy 3:1

The Bible gives us this powerful instruction:

> Make every effort to live in peace with everyone.
>
> Hebrews 12:14 NIV

In other words, people might slam their door on you, but you cannot slam the door on them. God invites us to see the world from a different perspective. My prayer is that God will renew the view of our purpose on earth as stalwart pillars that show others the way home. Even though the world might be shaking, we will stand fast. It will not always be easy.

> They will be divided, father against son and son against father, mother against daughter and daughter against mother, mother-in-law against daughter-in-law and daughter-in-law against mother-in-law.
>
> Luke 12:53 NIV

Indeed, these times will cause some close relationships to cease. But if we stand for the truth and refuse to vacillate, many will come around. There will be a day that God will speak to their hearts.

Remember, as Christians we are not called to stand *against* things as much as we are called to stand *for* Jesus. To be known for what you are against does no one any good. You can't lead your enemies to Christ. Only your friends.

And have you ever noticed that critics never build anything?

Don't forget who you are in these days. No neutrality. The world may change, but stay stalwart in your family and your home; not being belligerent, but stalwart; not being gullible, but teachable; not being arrogant, but courageous.

> **Jesus Christ never changes. Neither must we.**

Remember the story I told in chapter 3 about the rabbi who offered to pay a soldier to ask him every day, "Who are you and what are you doing here?"

Let me pose those same two questions to you: "Who are you and what are you doing here?" God has given each of us a purpose. Don't forget who you are. The world may change, but stay stalwart. Jesus Christ never changes. Neither must we.

Following Jesus

Diognetus was a Greek leader who wanted to learn about Christians who were new to his society. So he hired a researcher to look into the group.

Here are some excerpts of the researcher's letter to Diognetus, written around AD 100–150. It reminds us not of an era, but of a person that we must return to.

> Christians are not distinguished from the rest of the world by country or language or customs. They do not live in cities of their own. They do not use a peculiar form of speech, nor do they follow an eccentric manner of life. They live in their own countries, but they live only as aliens. They have a share in everything as citizens, but they endure all things as foreigners. They marry just like everyone else and they beget children, but they don't cast off their offspring. They share their meals with each

other, but not their marriage bed. It is true that they are in the flesh, but they do not live according to the flesh. They busy themselves on earth, but their citizenship is in heaven. . . .

While Christians are settled among corruptible things, they seem to wait for the incorruptibility that will be theirs in heaven. This is the post and the purpose that God has ordered for them when they seem to not be able to escape.[1]

The singleness of purpose was well known and easily observable. There was no mistaking the nature of a Christian in the world.

No fuzzy lines.

Nothing watered down.

No blurred edges.

No wondering and no confusion.

Finishing Well

Choose well and watch how God will use you in the long run for His glory. Short runs don't seem to count in life.

The long runs do.

Over my thirty-plus years in ministry, I have seen dozens of trends, and as soon as one thing is done, another big thing rolls in, promising more than its predecessor. But in the end, I have found that staying close to Jesus in a pure and simple way may not make you immune to problems, but it will make you last.

You have only one life to give. Learn to live it God's way. Walk on His side of the street and you won't collide with people as much. Take note not only of the fact that you've made a decision to follow Jesus Christ but also that you have made a decision about the attitude with which you will follow Him.

1. "The Epistle to Diognetus," in J.B. Lightfoot, Ed., and J.R. Harmer, Ed., *The Apostolic Fathers: Revised Texts With Short Introductions and English Translations* (Published by the Trustees of the Lightfoot Fund, 1891).

And one day you will hear Him say, "Well done, my good and faithful servant." When you hear that, you will be glad that you "loved Him more."

In changing times, we have a strong tendency to become distracted. Instead, stick with the purity and simplicity of devotion to Christ. Jesus offers us this refreshing faith. It's a safe haven when life spins out of control.

Let's get back to Jesus!

It's so simple and so pure. Don't stray from that. The enemy attempted to distract Eve, and he will do the same with us. Anything that is not pure and simple in our devotion to Jesus is subject to corruption.

It's time to get back to Jesus.

But I am afraid that, as the serpent deceived Eve by his craftiness, your minds will be led astray from the *simplicity and purity of devotion to Christ*.

2 Corinthians 11:3 (emphasis added)

1. What types of change have you experienced lately?

2. Can you identify some areas of neutrality starting to take place in the church today?

3. "Who are you and what are you doing here?" Why is it important to ask yourself these two questions every day? How would you answer them?

4. Why is the *posture* of how you stand for truth just as important as standing for truth?

5. We often don't like predictability, but there is a *beautiful predictability* about Jesus. Is that comforting or disturbing to you?

SPECIAL THANKS

Thank you to Andy McGuire and the team at Bethany House, agent Greg Johnson at the WordServe Literary Group, researcher Elaine Ohlson, and editor Marcus Brotherton.

And thank you to the many who have walked with me over the bumpy terrain in the kingdom of God. How often we wish it were smooth, but Jesus never promised us convenience; He promised His *presence*.

Thank you to my wife, Anna, who has been with me for over thirty-eight years. Thank you to our fabulous people in the New Hope network of churches all over the world. A special tip of my hat to Dan and Carol Ann Shima and George and Pat Iranon, who helped pioneer New Hope with me back in the old days. And a special thanks to Paul and Susie Lam, Dave and Yumi Yogi, John and Lanu Tilton, Rod and Becki Shimabukuro, and our staff, who have been so fantastic as we grew over the years. And I can never forget the saints of New Hope Hilo, where it all began: Pauline Spencer, Doris Aoki, Mary Hiyama, and many more who pioneered with me when I was only thirty-one.

The older you get, the more relationships mean to you. I turn sixty this year, and as I come to my final chapter, I look back and wish I would have loved Jesus and people more.

So with the rest of my days, that is what I shall do.

Won't you join me?

Wayne Cordeiro is senior pastor of New Hope Christian Fellowship in Oahu, Hawaii, which is listed as one of the top twenty-five most influential churches in America, and one of the top ten most innovative. He has been a pastor for ten years in Oregon and twenty-eight years in Hawaii.

Wayne is a church planter at heart and has been instrumental in planting more than 150 churches. Through New Hope International, the church planting division of the ministry, seventy of the churches have been established in the Pacific Rim countries of the Philippines, Japan, Australia, and Myanmar, as well as in Hawaii, California, Montana, Washington, and Nevada. At last count, more than 530,000 people have made first-time decisions for Christ through these churches.

New Hope in Hawaii is known by some as the largest shrinking mega-church in the nation, sending out nearly 12,000 congregants to begin over twenty-five daughter churches on the capital island of Oahu.

In addition to his responsibilities at New Hope Oahu, Wayne fulfills the role as chancellor over his alma mater, Eugene Bible College—now known as New Hope Christian College—in Eugene, Oregon. NHCC also has a Hawaii campus, along with two other Bible colleges in Myanmar and Japan. Wayne is an avid builder of emerging leaders. Through mentoring programs, internships, and leadership practicums, Wayne has spent much of his life developing the ministry potential of others.

Wayne has been a contributing author to a host of leadership magazines and was recently interviewed by the *New York Times*.

He has authored twelve books, including *Doing Church as a Team, Dream Releasers, Seven Rules of Success, Rising Above, Attitudes that Attract Success, Culture Shift, Divine Mentor, Leading on Empty, The Irresistible Church,* and *Sifted.* Wayne is also the author of the *Life Journal,* which is being used by thousands of churches worldwide in bringing people back to the Word of God and back to Jesus, pure and simple.

He enjoys water sports, riding his Harley, and training horses. Wayne and his wife, Anna, have been married for thirty-eight years. They have three married children, Amy, Aaron, and Abigail. Wayne and Anna enjoy their six grandchildren, who reside in Oregon and Hawaii.

More From
Wayne Cordeiro